...s never too late to find the courage to admit to yourself what tr...
...and then start to point the direction of your life
...towards it. Even if your action are small
... start, one day at a time and build from
... there.

© 2013, Lorna Jane Clarkson

Published by The Messenger Group Pty Ltd
PO Box H241
Australia Square NSW 1215
www.themessengergroup.com.au

A CIP catalogue of this book is available from the National
Library of Australia.

Clarkson, Lorna Jane
MORE
ISBN 978-0-9870974-5-3

□□□ LORNA JANE

Creative Director: Lorna Jane Clarkson
Creative Designer: Tara McCafferty
Food Editor: Rhiannon Mack
Food & MNB Styling: Ashleigh Hipwood
Food & MNB Photographers: Shaelah Ariotti, Louise Smit
Profile & Fashion Photographer: Jason Zambelli

www.lornajane.com.au
www.movenourishbelieve.com
Instagram: @ljclarkson
Twitter: @lornajaneactive

MO
RE

what is active living?

Active Living (ak-tiv liv-ing) – verb:

1. To live an inspirational active life. **2.** To actively engage in your life and live each day with purpose and intent. **3.** To challenge yourself in big and small ways and strive for more. **4.** To choose to surround yourself with positive people and influences. **5.** To build rituals into your day to keep you on course to achieving your goals. **6.** To nourish your body with deliciously wonderful clean food. **7.** To keep your blood pumping and mood lifted with regular exercise. **8.** To feed your mind and spirit with new learning and experiences. **9.** To nourish your relationships **10.** To have confidence in yourself that you can do whatever it is you truly believe in. **11.** To make every second of every day truly count. **12.** To leave a legacy to help make a positive difference in other people's lives.

Synonyms:

1. Believing. **2.** Exercising, keeping fit. **3.** Nourishing, eating healthy food. **4.** Taking time to do the things you love. **5.** Embracing new experiences. **6.** Being positive.

contents

BIG
THINGS
OFTEN
HAVE
SMALL
BEGINNINGS

contents

BECAUSE YOU WANTED
MORE.

I'm LORNA JANE:

*An ACTIVE woman, DESIGNER of my own active-wear range,
ACTIVE LIVING advocate, and I have to admit,
AN ETERNAL OPTIMIST.*

I have a history of 20 plus years in the fitness industry as
an instructor, gym owner, active-wear designer and all-time
lover of anything to do with health and working out.

And I have a confession to make:

I get this feeling when I'm around people, that
I somehow make them want to be fitter and
healthier. I can walk up to a group of women
and the topic of conversation automatically
changes to their eating habits, their latest
exercise routine or whatever's motivating them
to be more active.

They talk about their food and fitness
challenges, ask my advice, and question how
I manage to achieve everything I do in my life,
as well as stay fit and healthy on a daily basis.

And you know what, my answer is pretty
much always the same:

ACTIVE LIVING.

I have been Actively Living my life every day
now, for as long as I can remember; and I'm
not just talking about exercise.

Sure, exercise is an important part of my life,
but Active Living is so much MORE. It is a
combination of the physical, emotional and
psychological choices I make every day to
look, think and perform at my best in ALL
aspects of my life.

When practised every day, I believe Active
Living is the key to improving your life;
and when equipped with my Move Nourish
Believe philosophy it really is quite simple
to achieve.

this is the start of something MORE BEAUTIFUL.

this is the start of something MORE beautiful

I HAVE ALREADY ADMITTED TO BEING SLIGHTLY OBSESSED, but I need you to know that I am as passionate and committed to being the modern-day philosopher for Active Living as any environmental or rights campaigner. The truth is, I know first hand how amazing your life can become when you follow the Move Nourish Believe philosophy and that's why I have to share this message with as many people as I possibly can.

I want to empower women around the world to discover the rewards of being active, proactive participants in their lives, and not just bystanders distracted from doing the things they love by an endless stream of daily obligations or by subconsciously becoming a passenger in someone else's dream life.

I am asked questions about Active Living almost every day and that's why I decided to write this book, because it became increasingly clear you wanted MORE.

MORE recipes.
MORE ways to move.
MORE inspiration to keep you motivated on your active journey.
MORE information on Active Living and the things that I do
        in my life to be at my best every day.

If you have already begun your active journey this book will give you more information, ideas and inspiration to encourage you along the way. And if you aren't already living an active life, through this book I hope to show you what you've been missing, and just how enriched and fulfilling your life can be.

For those who are already familiar with the Lorna Jane Move Nourish Believe philosophy, you'll know that it is a daily practise.

But did you know it was the key to Active Living?

more recipes. more ways to move. more inspiration to keep yo
MORE OF THE FIT WOMAN'S SECRETS 13.
otivated on your active journey. more information on acti

So let's get clear on Active Living
because it can mean so many things to us at
different times in our lives. Active Living is...

*Building rituals into your day
to keep you on course to achieving
your goals.*

Nourishing your body with wonderful food.

*feeding your mind and spirit
with new learnings and experiences.*

living each day with
purpose and intent.

MOVE. NOURISH. BELIEVE.

Challenging yourself in big and small ways to strive for more.

Making every second of every day truly count.

Choosing to surround yourself with positive people and influences

Having confidence in yourself that you can do whatever it is you truly believe in.

Never Give Up

Keeping your blood pumping and mood lifted with regular movement.

And so much MORE.

I'm here to tell you that by practising Active Living on a daily basis you can absolutely transform your life into one that will see you jumping out of bed in the morning with an enthusiasm for each day that you'd only ever dreamed of. And a simple way of approaching each day that will give you a purpose in life that goes beyond monetary reward, and ultimately creates a more uplifting, balanced and joyous life.

As I sat down to write this book it became glaringly obvious that this new project had to go beyond Move Nourish Believe and define Active Living in more detail.

So then I started thinking about all the questions that I hadn't answered with my first book. I asked customers, friends and members of my team what MORE they needed to know about Active Living.

I found that you wanted a deeper, more personal insight into the MOVE NOURISH BELIEVE philosophy (and subsequently Active Living) that has made me a better designer, businesswoman, wife, friend - in fact an all round better person.

So think of this book as me sharing my life - my stories, my inspirations and personal experiences, the food I love, the things I do every day, the things I never do, and the things I do now and again — with the hope that it will inspire you to live your best, most fulfilling active life.

I PROMISE

to be authentic and speak from the heart, as well as give you insights into my daily rituals, how I run my business and motivate myself to eat well and exercise every single day of my life. I am humbled by the thought that you loved my first book and have asked for MORE and am so excited because I have so much MORE to share with you on Active Living and all things Move Nourish Believe.

SO HERE IS MY

MORE

YOUR ACTIVE LIFE STARTS NOW.

For me, the beginning of my Active Living journey and one of the most life-changing decisions I ever made, was 23 years ago when I made the commitment to live authentically:

To be ME and live my life as I had always dreamt it could be.

This decision meant letting go of many old habits and anything not in line with who I truly wanted to be. I gave up trying to change myself in order to win the approval of others, let go of any negative thoughts that could hold me back and decided to be fearless and live my life guided by the things that mattered the most to me.

But the biggest step of all was when I decided to follow my natural strengths and talents and start pursuing the work I loved. That's when I took that great big leap of faith, quit my day job and started LORNA JANE.

> "There is no doubt that each of us is born an individual.
> Why is it then that so many of us die carbon copies?"
> - Jodie Foster

It's not as if I had consciously been pretending to be someone else for the first half of my life, but I was too compromising. I was taking the easy road and behaving like everyone else around me. Don't get me wrong, I was happy, but there was this nagging feeling I was supposed to be doing something else, that I was missing out on something, that my life should be bigger.

COURAGE.

How we spend our days is ultimately how we spend our lives and I knew in my heart that the purpose of my life had to be so much more than what I was currently doing day in, day out.

It felt like I was caught up in the busy-ness of things that really weren't important to me and had forgotten what I valued most in life. That's when I knew I couldn't ignore it anymore, I had to change my life and start afresh.

Stepping out of my comfort zone, starting my own business and having the courage to forgo the security of a full-time job was scary, and I had to think long and hard

about it before I was comfortable with the decision. But I think life-changing moments always feel like that; you come to a crossroad and you have to make honest decisions about your future and ultimately take responsibility for your life and where it is going.

For me, these decisions were made so much easier when I worked out what I wanted to do with my life, what my values were and what my purpose was in life.

I don't believe it is good enough to just do something that you think you are good at, or that you have some interest in. You owe it to yourself to find a way to do what you love.

Finding your purpose can be as simple as asking yourself what you are passionate about, what you love to do and what it is in your life that you can't stop thinking about. Then you take that one thing that you are really passionate about and find a way to make it a bigger part of your life every day.

Your comfort zone

Active Living
Where the magic happens.

authentic best self

It's never too late to admit to yourself what truly makes you happy, connect with what that might be, and then start to point the direction of your life towards it. Even if you just make small changes to start, one day at a time and build from there. I did it when I was 25. I had a mortgage and other financial commitments that I could easily have used as excuses to keep doing the same old thing (riding the hamster wheel), but I am so glad I didn't!

I decided that life was too short to live with regret and if things didn't work out as planned I could always come back to my current life. At least I could say I had given it a go, gone out on a limb and tried!

Living authentically is about allowing yourself to be driven by your heart, not your head. When we live without purpose we often feel lost and confused. We may become easily discouraged and struggle

to make decisions about the right thing to do so we do nothing – our life stands still. Connecting with your purpose provides clarity, a sense of direction and powerful motivation.

It's also about celebrating your individuality and realising you won't be great at anything unless you feel great about yourself and the unique talents and ideas you have to offer the world. Be true to your beliefs, live by your own code and above all, dare to voice your original thoughts and opinions.

At times being authentic can be intimidating and requires letting go of so many things that you are used to doing, while embracing what is new and unfamiliar. But trust me, by connecting with your purpose you will discover a new sense of meaning in your life and understand the *why* in all that you do.

My personal why is to inspire women towards Active Living, and how I do this every day is with my Move Nourish Believe philosophy, and by designing amazing active wear that motivates you to be active.

So ask yourself – am I doing what I love? What do I value in life? What is my purpose?

Today could be the first day of your new life. Take it from me – once you discover your purpose in life and experience the fulfilment and happiness that comes from living authentically, you won't waste one more second of your precious life living any other way!

"ONE DAY YOUR LIFE WILL FLASH BEFORE YOUR EYES, MAKE SURE IT'S WORTH WATCHING."

- Gerard Way

I recently read a book that talked about how our total time on this planet was an average of 30,000 days ...

JUST 30,000 DAYS!

That seemed an alarmingly small number to me and I became a bit fixated on counting them. I began to value each day so much more, and was even more determined to make every second count.

It's really surprising how something as simple as turning a page in a book and reading a comment can reignite your commitment to achieving your goals, big or small, just by realising the importance of time, how little we actually have of it and how quickly it can pass us by if we're not paying attention.

imagine

Another way to look at it is to imagine that every day your bank credits your account with $86,400, but every evening deletes the amount you failed to use. What would you do? Spend every cent of course!

Well you have such a bank account – but instead of money the currency is time.

Every day it credits you with 86,400 seconds, and at midnight, whatever you have failed to use, is lost. The balance is not carried over to the next day, and overdrafts are not permitted. Each day the bank called 'time' opens a new account for you and burns the records of the day before. If you fail to use the day's seconds, they are lost forever.

So what do you intend to do with your precious 30,000 days worth of 86,400 seconds? If you're anything like me: I say let's savour every single second, minute and hour of each and every day. Dream, achieve and do more to make our time on this planet count.

I already know my purpose and why I am here. But thinking about how precious time is and how little time we have to do everything made me want to step things up a little.
So if you feel the same, start by making a list of all the things you would like to have, do, or be - so that you can have a clear vision of what you want to achieve and then start setting some goals.

We can choose to do anything, but not everything in life - that's why it's important to know your priorities. Every now and then, stop to ask yourself: "What really matters to me?" Then ask yourself: "Am I spending my precious time on the things that really matter - the things I value the most? Or am I living someone else's dreams and priorities?"

All goals and achievements spring from having intent. Without intention, we can find ourselves wandering through life without direction. Having a list of what you want to achieve makes each day more meaningful; it makes each day and every second count towards the bigger picture.

I believe it's essential to start each day with a plan. Rather than just letting stuff happen, having a to-do list gives you a reason to jump out of bed in the morning, goals that give you something to achieve each day and more control over how your day, weeks and life in general unfolds.

Your intentions don't have to be earth-shattering but as simple as "I am going to have an enjoyable and productive day." You might even set an intention for different phases of your day, such as:

WORK

"I am well prepared for the big meeting. If I am asked difficult questions, I will take a breath and answer as best as I can. I will do well."

WORKOUT

"I will be stronger than my excuses today."

MEETING A FRIEND

"I will really enjoy this chance to make a difference in their day."

MAKING DINNER

"I will cook a healthy and nutritious meal for my family tonight and celebrate how fortunate we are to have each other, our health and our happiness."

...or your intention may indeed be a life-changing one, to finally embark on that project you believe will transform your life.

In my life plan I have so much that I want to do. Knowing I've already used up about half of my 30,000 days has made me feel that I have to giddy-up if I want to get everything done and achieve all that I want in my life.

It reinforced how truly important it was for me, when my time was up (how depressing…) that I would have managed in my own way to make a difference.

I want to leave my mark; a legacy if you like, and be remembered for inspiring women and advocating Active Living around the world. It can seem quite daunting at times but I have learnt that achieving great things can be as simple as putting one foot in front of the other, making good decisions every day and then over time you look up and you've arrived (that's how it happened with my life and successes anyway!).

But I still have so many more mountains to climb and things I want to achieve. And that's what I love about life: there are so many opportunities; you just have to look up and find them.

– BE UNREASONABLE –

STRIVE FOR MORE

Remember when we were kids, full of hope, curiosity and creative rebellion? Our imagination knew no boundaries, we broke the rules and we weren't afraid to strive for more – we weren't afraid to be unreasonable in the pursuit of what we wanted!

The world was built by people who weren't afraid to be unreasonable, to make change happen and constantly strive to achieve and be more. Some people might suggest that striving for more is unhealthy and can possibly lead to unhappiness and discontent. Others believe we are built to push beyond our comfort zones to reach for something higher; to be EXTRAORDINARY.

My belief is that we are here to shine. I believe that with every part of my being. You are here to find that cause, that main aim that will have you jumping out of bed in the morning with that child-like fire in your belly. You are meant to find something that your life will stand for, that will consume you, something so beautiful that you will have to share it with the rest of the world.

It is so important to constantly challenge yourself, play a bigger game and use your creative talents. This is our destiny and what we were meant to do. But it doesn't have to be all work and no play and definitely doesn't mean that we can't have our fair share of fun along the way.

Time is too short and too wonderful to waste on mundane things. You are here on earth for a reason – say yes to the people and things in your life you should say yes to. Find your own personal reason to exist and work out a way to live it in your life with balance.

**YOUR LIFE
IS YOUR MESSAGE
TO THE WORLD.
MAKE SURE IT IS
INSPIRING**

Every day counts, so keep growing; changing until you find your own perfect balance between the outstanding achievement and fulfilment you want out of life and all the crazy enjoyment and celebration you need along the way.

I know this now, but there have been times in my career, especially in the early days when I really lost the concept of balance, and I have to admit it didn't feel great. I was spending a lot of time chasing my dreams but not finding enough time to escape the stresses of running a business to relax and re-energise. I even found myself wondering if pursuing my dream was worth it when I didn't actually feel like I was living the dream at all! I had become way too single-minded, focusing on the destination instead of enjoying each day and celebrating each milestone along the way.

It really is equally important, for a successful and balanced life, to enjoy the view as we travel forward, and be grateful for everything and everyone in our lives right now.
I soon came to realise that life is a journey of growth and development, full of obstacles as well as celebration and you should make the time to savour every part of it. Don't make the same mistake that I made - take time to smell the roses, be sure to appreciate what you have and find time for the people in your life that are important.

But also remember, that shouldn't be an excuse that stops you from striving for what you want, because your dreams and being extraordinary are the most important thing!

We know that our time on earth is a journey to be savoured so inhabit the moments and remember to enjoy every step of this adventure we call life, but don't for one minute take your eyes off what you want to achieve.

SETTING GOALS FOR
SUCCESS

Imagine what your life would be like if you were living at 100 per cent of your potential.

Most of us are being pulled in so many different directions that it's often hard to be clear on what we want out of life and whether we are even heading in the right direction.

I've found the key is to make sure you check in with your values and really think about what matters to YOU the most. Then decide where and how you want to focus your energy by setting some goals. By making a commitment to your goals and what you really want to achieve, you are putting yourself in the best possible position to make your dream life become a reality.

It is so important to set goals for yourself because if you haven't set goals in your life then how can you possibly hope to attain them? Goals motivate us, help us get clarity, and point us in the right direction towards bigger and better things. And the more often you remind yourself of your goals, the more your mind will work, consciously and subconsciously, on ways to achieve them.

BUT REMEMBER:

Setting goals is just the beginning. You then have to formulate a plan to get there, one step at a time.

I've found that when you make a decision about what you want and begin focusing on achieving a specific goal, you will also find your subconscious goes to work. And it's a powerful ally. You will be amazed at some of the new ideas that pop into your head and how you will come up with innovative solutions to problems or obstacles that would usually get in your way.

Sometimes having a big plan and ambitious goals can be daunting, as well as exciting. So when it feels like life is putting obstacle after obstacle in your path, the most important thing to remember is why you began this journey in the first place and not to give up. Every so often you may need to dust yourself off, adjust your plan or revise your strategy. But whatever you do, don't ever lose sight of your *why,* the reason you started down this road in the first place; because you had a dream.

I think we like to complicate things when it really is quite simple; find what it is that makes you happy and who it is that makes you happy and make them a bigger part of your life. Remember to focus on the dream that you are working towards and how amazing you will feel when you achieve it. Goals promote personal growth, they breathe life into our days and inspire us to be better and achieve more. Setting goals is an investment in your dreams and a statement that you are committed to achieving them.

"Dreams are fun to talk about, but when dreams are turned into goals they become possible. And when goals are turned into plans they become real."

Anthony Robbins

HERE ARE SOME TIPS ON MAKING YOUR GOALS (STICK)

1

WHEN YOU ARE REALLY CLEAR ABOUT SOMETHING YOU WANT TO ACHIEVE, WRITE IT DOWN AND REFER BACK TO IT REGULARLY. PERHAPS PROMISE YOURSELF A REWARD WHEN YOU HAVE REACHED YOUR GOAL.

2

SHARE YOUR GOAL WITH SOMEONE YOU TRUST. YOUR HUSBAND OR PARTNER, A GOOD FRIEND OR BUSINESS ASSOCIATE, EVEN A PROFESSIONAL MENTOR WHO WILL BE SUPPORTIVE AND KEEP YOUR PROGRESS ON TRACK.

3

IDEALLY, SET YOURSELF A TIME LIMIT FOR ACHIEVING THE GOAL. IT WILL MOTIVATE YOU MORE.

4

DO SOMETHING EVERY DAY THAT REITERATES COMMITMENT TO YOUR GOAL.

5

WHEN YOU HAVE REACHED YOUR GOAL, CONGRATULATE YOURSELF FOR HAVING DONE WHAT YOU SAID YOU WOULD. GIVE YOURSELF THAT REWARD. IT'S EVEN MORE IMPORTANT TO ACKNOWLEDGE YOURSELF THAN GETTING RECOGNITION FROM OTHER PEOPLE.

6

BUILD ON YOUR ACHIEVEMENT BY SETTING ANOTHER GOAL. STRIVE FOR MORE

the IMPORTANCE *of* Rituals

The way I look at it, your days are your life in miniature. What you do today is actually creating your future. The words you speak, the thoughts you think, the food you eat, and the actions you take are defining your destiny, shaping who you are and what your life will stand for.

For me there is no such thing as an unimportant day when you want to have a wonderful life and achieve great things, and that's why I believe building rituals into your day are extremely important; taking little steps every day towards being a fitter, healthier, more positive and successful version of who you were the day before.

Life moves quickly. Your days become weeks, then months and, before you know it, another year has passed you by. Let it be a year of growth and improvement, not a year of standing still (or, indeed, going backwards).

One of the most important and beneficial daily rituals I do for myself is rise early (usually around 5.30am) and take a couple of hours each morning for myself.

I stretch and spend some time thinking, exercise, body brush and shower. I never look at e-mails before this. And then I have a delicious, healthy breakfast and catch up on the news, what happened with our US business overnight, emails and any other pressing business and personal matters. I try not to start my day at full speed because I find allowing myself that all-important 'me time' in the morning makes me a better person for the rest of the day.

RITUALS

I also make sure that I find time every day to walk with my dog, Roger, and have some quality time with my husband, Bill. Reading is also something I don't go a day without, even if it's just a few pages before I go to sleep at night. These are all things that are important to me and have become a non-negotiable part of my day. Sometimes it can be difficult to fit them in as well as everything else that the day brings; AND THAT IS WHY I HAVE MADE THEM MY RITUALS.

Top athletes know that practice is how you get to greatness. So if you want to live a certain way, creating rituals that support the lifestyle you want, incorporating all the things you know will make you better and bring you closer to your goals, is a good way to start.

But remember, the whole point of rituals is to make sure you find time to do the things you should be doing, but also the things that you love.

It's important that you make these daily practices something you look forward to, so they enrich your life and you will actually want to do them.

Find your own series of rituals and perform them with consistency. Don't make excuses to skip them when you're too busy or circumstances aren't absolutely ideal. Just make it work! When you travel, for instance, look at it as an opportunity to find MORE time to spend doing the things you love, or a chance to try new ways to exercise, discover local health food cafes, or buy some new books to inspire your reading.

That's not to say you won't, for instance, sleep late, skip an exercise session once in a while or eat a little too much chocolate. But as you continue to practise, your attitude gradually shifts, your rituals become habits and you'll begin to see the rewards and positive change that regular rituals can bring.

In fact you will soon find that good habits are as addictive as bad ones, and that sticking to your rituals will help you achieve so much more from your day, and as a result, your life.

Rituals matter

YOUR SCHEDULE
DOESN'T LIE.

Don't just talk about it - BE ABOUT IT

Talk is cheap. Show me your schedule (or diary) and I'll show you what your priorities are!

I guess this goes back to living an authentic life and checking in on your values. We can quite often think and say that our priorities are one thing, but in reality find that we put all of our obligations before them and actually run out of time to do the things that matter the most to us.

So many people say they value their health and fitness above all else, but I don't see any runs or gym sessions scheduled in their diaries. And then there's the "my family comes first" comment from executives who have business meetings in their calendar from 8am till 7.30pm.

Now, I don't want to sit here and criticise, but what I do want to say is that there is no authentic success or lasting happiness if your daily schedule is misaligned with your deepest values.

Your schedule is the best barometer for what you truly value and believe is important in life. So really think about what you value the most, what you want to spend more time doing and literally schedule it into your life.

Make an appointment with yourself or a friend to do some regular exercise. Organise a movie night with your family or simply book yourself in for a massage once a month.

I have been living authentically with the Move Nourish Believe philosophy for such a long time now but I STILL schedule in my workouts, important time with my family and friends as well as massages, movie nights, time to think and any other MNB appointments that I would like to keep.

So test yourself. Make a list of what matters the most to you, then make a list of everything you did last week – and compare the lists. Then make the changes you need for the following week to do more in your life of what truly matters to YOU!

Keep doing this week after week until the lists match and you are actually living what you value and love.

Walk your talk and see what a difference it can make when you commit to what you love to do as part of your schedule. It also gives you something to look forward to when you are looking at all the other 'not so fun things' that you may need to get through during your day.

Why i live to work.

Find your THING and do that THING better than anyone else does it, even if you think that THING has no value, because I promise you that it does. And I promise you that other people will see this value too.

i love to travel, i love to run, i love spending time with inspiring people, i love collecting and sharing inspiring words, i love work,

i love

what I do, and consider myself extremely fortunate to be able to merge all the things in life that I am really passionate about, into my career, as well as a wonderful life. I had a dream to wake up every day passionate about how I was living my life and now that dream is a reality.

*i love the weekends,
i love inspiring meetings,
i love customer feedback,
i love time with my dog and
i love designing active wear.*

My business and personal life is so intimately intertwined it is honestly a little difficult to separate them. I work with my husband and we promote our personal philosophy for life (Move Nourish Believe) within our company and to our customers. This philosophy encompasses so many of my personal passions that I find it difficult to differentiate between my passions within and outside of my business.

I am passionate about being fit and healthy, and anything to do with these subjects interests me. I love to try new exercise concepts, read about breakthroughs in sports and nutrition and I collect healthy recipes almost every day.

I GUESS WHAT I'M TRYING TO SAY HERE IS THAT...

i love what i do.

I have designed a life that enables me to wake up every day and appreciate the fun, the lesson and the sense of achievement in everything I do … whether I am in the office or at home on the weekend.

People often ask me how I manage my work/life balance and to be quite honest I think that when your life is driven by passion and the urge to make a difference, any thought of having to separate what you do for a living and what you love disappears. It is only those that don't enjoy their work or haven't yet found their purpose in life who have to even think about it.

I love my work because it is my life. I have found my purpose: to inspire women to live their best life through Active Living. I can't just switch it on during business hours and then forget about it while I'm at home. When you are really passionate about something, it just doesn't work like that. Not for me anyway!

I firmly believe advocating Active Living is the reason I'm here. It's what drives me to do, and be, better every day. It may have started off just being about the active wear, but today it is so much MORE.

I also get to work with an amazing team of inspiring women who share my passion for Active Living and are united in our love of all things Move Nourish Believe. It makes every day a joy. It honestly doesn't feel like work and I have to pinch myself sometimes to believe that I actually get paid to do this!

There are so many reasons why I love my work but one of the standouts for me is when I meet Lorna Jane customers and they share their stories. There are stories about weight loss, overcoming illness, about inspirational quotes being the strength they needed to get them through difficult times, and so much MORE.

I know for some people who are new to Lorna Jane, the idea that an active-wear brand can change people's lives and inspire them to do great things could sound a little nutty.

But over the years, Lorna Jane and our Move Nourish Believe philosophy has become so much MORE to our customers. We are a sisterhood, a support system and kindred spirits on all things fitness and fashion. We are a rich source of knowledge on health and fitness. We share recipes, new exercise routines and things that inspire us.

We have become part of your daily lives and think of you as a friend. This is just another reason that I love my work. I'm emotionally engaged and I can't imagine my life without my customers, my team and this wonderful way of life we have created.

BEING FIT is the BEST

Feeling

I HAVE BEEN *FIT* AND
HEALTHY FOR AS LONG AS
I CAN REMEMBER, BECAUSE
QUITE HONESTLY I DON'T
KNOW ANY OTHER WAY TO
LIVE MY LIFE.

*I am very clear on the importance of
having a good diet, exercising regularly and
keeping a positive mindset because I believe
the key to successful living is living well
every day.*

IN KEEPING WITH MY MOVE NOURISH BELIEVE PHILOSOPHY

I PROMISE TO;

MOVE my body every day
– letting every single cell know I'm alive.

NOURISH from the inside out, with not
only nutritious foods, but by finding time
to do the things I love.

Truly BELIEVE anything is possible if
I'm willing to work for it.

Being fit and healthy is about having an abundance of energy. It's about feeling fit, strong and alive. Exercise is also instantly invigorating and a great stress reducer. It's vital for long-term health and wellbeing, and can improve your mental powers by 20-30 per cent.

There are many benefits to regular exercise and without a doubt you have a better chance of being successful and fulfilled in your life if you are in good physical shape. Exercise has been proven to lift your confidence, and is definitely a great way to clear your mind, revitalise your body, and alleviate the stresses of everyday life.

The key to staying committed is to find ways to exercise that you enjoy, and that you respond well to, both mentally and physically.

Fun is the key word here, and you have to find a way to exercise that you enjoy if you expect to do it every day.

For me it's a combination of strength training, yoga and cardio. The strength training shapes my body, the yoga keeps me flexible and the cardio keeps me fit and stops me from gaining weight.

Finding the time and different ways to move my body are non-negotiable rituals I practise every day. And if I'm totally honest, one of the reasons why is because I don't feel quite the same if I don't.

Strength training is an important part of my routine and I do two one-and-a-half hour sessions a week with my trainer. I find not only does this routine keep me strong and toned but I have fewer injuries and can perform better in life. Even if I'm travelling I try not to miss this part of my regimen; the sessions won't be as intense as when my coach is beside me of course, but it keeps me from slipping too far behind for when I get home.

yoga

is the
ULTIMATE
stress buster

If strength training is something I do to look good, then yoga is what I do to make myself FEEL GOOD. I do yoga every day, mostly on my own at home and then two or three times a week in a more structured class format.

It's a place I can go to lose mobile phone reception, forget the things on my to-do list and return to the simplicity of being in the moment and breathing.

There is a reason they call yoga 'the fitness fountain of youth'. I find it strengthens and lengthens my body, clears my mind, and opens up my perspective. It also teaches us to breathe really deeply and properly which promotes the distribution of oxygen to all areas of our body.

One of the other amazing benefits of yoga that most people overlook is the inspiring and uplifting insights that our yoga instructors share with us. They remind us that we are perfect just the way we are, that

life is to be enjoyed and embraced, and that acceptance and belief in ourselves is the ultimate key to strength and beauty. Which is further proof that the success of yoga and the reason so many of us love it – doesn't just lie in our ability to perform postures but in how it positively changes the ways we think about ourselves and live our lives.

I like to do cardio at least two to three times a week. It can be anything from stair runs, a hike in a local park or a run on the treadmill, as long as it gets my heart racing and my blood really pumping. Sometimes if my schedule is really full and I don't have much time I will just jump on the treadmill after walking my dog and do a quick interval training session for 15-30 minutes or whatever time permits.

The rest of the time I just try to move my body as much as I can in everything I do.
I do my own heavy lifting, I run up the stairs instead of walking, I put a little extra
energy into everything I do and I go on active holidays rather than ones
that find me lazing by the pool all day.

It would be extremely rare for me to miss more than one day of exercise – and that's because
I like how good exercise makes me feel; but I'm not going to bash myself up or make myself
feel guilty if I miss a workout.

Sometimes life gets in the way - you might get a-once-in-a-lifetime opportunity to
hang-glide over the Sunshine Coast or simply have to stay back at work to meet a deadline.
Either way, exercise can be left for another day. I simply promise myself to work
twice as hard tomorrow.

the JOYS of READING

Reading, in my opinion, is one of the best disciplines you can practise on a daily basis to think and be at your best.

A great book by someone who is an expert in their field is like having a conversation with the author. It allows you to absorb some of their brilliance and possibly apply it to your own life.

Want to hang out with *Steve Jobs* or *Jane Fonda*? Have your morning coffee with *Richard Branson*? Try reading their books! Read about the people who inspire you, things you love, the things that make you laugh, the things you want to learn more about, or whatever you feel you need to escape the stresses of your day.

I have loved reading from a very early age, and still have fond memories of *Enid Blyton's* books, as well as *The Lion, the Witch and the Wardrobe* and classics such as *Alice in Wonderland* and *the Wizard of Oz*. I have no doubt that my early love of reading is what helped develop my creative thinking that would later develop into the desire to

design beautiful things. Reading also allowed me to experience other worlds outside of my own and sparked my imagination to believe in a life for me that could be just a little less ordinary.

I usually have a couple of books going at the same time and read them depending on what I feel I need at a particular time. One of the great things about books is that they are there for you whenever you need them and are a constant source of knowledge and support.

I can't imagine a day without reading, and my advice if you don't already have a love of reading is to give it a try; invest in your future and make the time to read something that inspires and nourishes you every day. What better way to learn new things and fill your mind with big ideas and dreams for your future!

"BOOKS ARE A DRUG WITH NO DANGER OF AN OVERDOSE. I AM THE HAPPY VICTIM OF BOOKS."

~Karl Lagerfeld

the SWEETEST THING

Whilst we are on the subject of things I love, I feel I should share with you that my all-time favourite food indulgence would have to be – and I guess always has been – CHOCOLATE.

It's probably not something you would expect me to say, but having a little chocolate is an important part of my active life because it's something that I truly love and want to experience every day.

Most of the time it's simply a chocolate protein shake before or after my workout but, when the cravings get a little crazy I find that just two squares of good quality dark chocolate or a piece of my homemade chocolate bark is enough to keep me happy.

Let's just say I am willing to work out longer and harder if it means I can enjoy just a little chocolate at the end of my day!

I think it's a shame when women feel guilty about enjoying such a wonderful treat. But that's the whole point – chocolate is a treat, not something you eat all the time in huge quantities.

If you nourish yourself with a healthy diet and move your body every day then choosing to reward yourself now and again with just a little is to be applauded.

> *I refuse to feel guilty about anything I decide to do. Once I have made a decision*
> *(and this includes eating chocolate) then I OWN that decision.*

If we are talking about chocolate in particular, I say enjoy every single moment of your chocolaty indulgence with absolutely no guilt attached. As far as I'm concerned, if I thought I was going to feel guilty then I wouldn't have decided to have it in the first place.

In fact, I've found that if I have a little 'fix' daily as part of a healthy diet, I'm far less likely to go on a chocolate binge, which is so much more detrimental to my health and my waistline.

If this still hasn't convinced you that chocolate is something to be relished, not regretted, here are some of my go-to recipes that will ensure you get all of the antioxidants (five-and-a-half times more than blueberries!) and health benefits that good quality chocolate can bring without all the hidden nasties.

chocolate & pumpkin
- - - - - - - - - - - - - -
brownies

Makes 15 serves
Prep time: 3 – 12 hrs
Cook time: 15 mins

2 cups pumpkin
(any variety)
4 cups almond meal
1 cup dates
½ tsp bi-carb soda
¼ cup cacao powder

2 free-range eggs
100g dark chocolate
(see chocolate bark
recipe to make your
own, or use any
commercial variety)

Puree the pumpkin, by steaming chopped
pumpkin until soft, mashing, and suspending it in
a sieve lined with clean muslin. Let the pumpkin
hang overnight, or for at least an hour, then
gently squeeze out any excess liquid.

Preheat oven to 160°C and line a baking tray
with baking paper.

Slowly melt chocolate in a heat-proof bowl over
a pot of slowly simmering water. Make sure the
bowl is not touching the water. Stir frequently.

In a saucepan on medium heat, 'melt' the dates
with a tablespoon or two of water. Stir frequently.
Once soft, take off the heat and add the bi-carb.
Stir and allow to foam.

Now mix all ingredients thoroughly in a bowl.

Spread onto lined baking tray and cook for 12-15
mins in 160°C oven. Brownies are cooked when
firm, but still extremely moist. Refrigerate the
brownies for at least 2 hrs before portioning.

chocolate-stuffed
- - - - - - - - - - - -
raspberries

Makes 2-4 serves   Prep time: 20 mins

¼ cup dark chocolate (see chocolate
bark recipe to make your own, or use any
commercial variety)
1 punnet raspberries (250g)

Slowly melt chocolate in a heat-proof bowl
over a pot of slowly simmering water. Make
sure the bowl is not touching the water.

Stir frequently.

While chocolate is melting, put the
raspberries in the freezer for a few mins.

Once melted, using a teaspoon or piping
bag, gently fill the centre of each raspberry
with chocolate.

Place in the fridge or freezer to set.

chocolate bark

Makes 20 serves
Prep time: 40 mins
Cook time: 10 mins

1 cup cacao butter, finely chopped
½ cup cacao powder
¼ -½ cup honey or maple syrup
(depending on taste)

Place cacao butter into a heat-proof bowl ove a pot of slowly simmering water.

Make sure the bowl is not touching the water.

Take the bowl off the pot when cacao butter is melted.

Stir through the cacao powder and sweetener.

2 tbsp sunflower seeds	2 tbsp goji berries
2 tbsp pumpkin seeds	2 tbsp dried blueberri
¼ cup almonds	¼-½ tsp finely ground
¼ cup shredded coconut	sea salt (depending on taste)

In a 150°C oven toast the seeds, almonds and coconut for around 10mins, or until they have slightly browned and are fragrant.

Let cool for 10 mins before adding the berries and salt. Stir through melted chocolate.

Spread over lined baking tray and place in the freezer. Once set, break up the bark into small pieces.

chocolate mint tea

Makes 2 serves
Prep time: 5 mins

2 sprigs mint leaves
3 tbsp cacao nibs
2 cups boiling water

Bring water to the boil in kettle or pot. Add the mint and cacao and allow to infuse for a few mins before straining and drinking.

believing is everything.

believe
and you will achieve

Keep your dreams alive.
Understand that to achieve anything
requires faith and belief in yourself, vision,
hard work, determination and dedication.
Remember all things are possible for those who believe.

THE POWER OF
POSITIVITY

If there is something - anything you want to achieve in life, the first and most important step is to decide to back yourself. Make the decision to believe in yourself and your dreams unconditionally and do whatever it takes to make those dreams a reality.

In my opinion, having a positive outlook is the key to having a happy and successful life, and one of the most important parts of that is having a 'fall down and get back up' attitude. Because let's face it, life has a habit of throwing obstacles in our way, and if we don't learn to dust ourselves off after a setback and get on with it, we're not going to get anywhere.

I also believe you can't live a positive life with a negative mindset. When you decide to be more positive, and adopt a positive frame of mind, it is only then that everything in life seems easier. That includes fitting exercise into your daily routine and caring enough about yourself

and your future self to invest time and energy into nourishing your body so you can give yourself a better future.

"SURROUND YOURSELF ONLY WITH PEOPLE WHO ARE GOING TO LIFT YOU HIGHER."

~Oprah Winfrey

Being positive is easier when you surround yourself with like-minded, positive people. So be mindful of the company you keep. Spend time with people who are supportive of your ambitions and who encourage you to be the best you can be.

In your personal life, and at work, you're only going to be as good as the people you spend time with. So be strong enough to let go of those who keep weighing you down, and make the decision to spend most of your time with people who are as passionate as you are about the plans you have for your life.

When you free yourself from negative people, you free yourself to be the best version of you. So make the choice to be with people you are proud to know, friends you admire, who love and respect you, people who make your day a little brighter simply by being in it.

BE

YOUR

BEAUTIFUL

SELF

Head office huddle

It is often commented on when people visit the Lorna Jane Head Office for the first time, how positive all of the people who work for us are and how amazing the energy is in the building. We also get so many compliments on the girls in-store, and how their positivity can really make a difference to our customers and how they feel for the rest of the day.

This is a great testament to what we have built at Lorna Jane and something I am extremely proud to be part of and to think it all started because I simply wanted to spend my days with positive like-minded people that shared my passion for ACTIVE LIVING.

YOUR CUSTOMERS ROCK

BEING POSITIVE IS AN ESSENTIAL INGREDIENT FOR ACTIVE LIVING.

So walk with the DREAMERS, the BELIEVERS, the COURAGEOUS, the CHEERFUL, the PLANNERS, the DOERS, and the SUCCESSFUL people with their heads in the clouds and their feet on the ground. Let their SPIRIT IGNITE A FIRE within you to BELIEVE that anything is possible; then go out and MAKE IT HAPPEN.

BE THE BEST VERSION OF you
move nourish believe
Lx

office meeting room wall

Keep your dream... have
faith and belief in yourself, vision, hard work determination
and dedication. Remember all things are possible for those that

Positive Affirmations

I have been collecting positive words and affirmations for as long as I can remember and the inspirational singlets that I print them on have been in our business since ... well, FOREVER.

I can't really explain the reasons why I love them so much except that they make me feel good and I feel the need to share this happiness by emailing them, sharing them on Instagram and Twitter, or printing them on a singlet to motivate your workouts.

HERE ARE 10 OF MY FAVOURITES
that I find myself using to inspire myself and
that you will often hear in the corridors at
Lorna Jane. I hope they will inspire you.

"DANCE LIKE NO ONE IS WATCHING."

"BE THE CHANGE
YOU WANT TO SEE IN THE WORLD."

"YOU CAN HAVE EVERYTHING,
JUST NOT EVERYTHING AT ONCE."

"DREAM, BELIEVE, ACHIEVE."

"BE SO GOOD THEY CAN'T IGNORE YOU."

"DON'T GIVE UP ON WHAT YOU WANT MOST,
FOR WHAT YOU WANT NOW."

"THINK DIFFERENTLY."

"BE YOUR OWN KIND OF BEAUTIFUL."

"MAKE IT HAPPEN."

And of course it goes without saying:

"NEVER, NEVER, NEVER GIVE UP."

Every day you will come across sayings or ideas that strike a chord, ignite your imagination or simply motivate you to think or be better. Whenever you see or hear something that really resonates with you and your dreams, jot it down. Create your own collection of positive affirmations and share them with the people you care about to help them on their journey too.

"Keep your THOUGHTS POSITIVE
because your thoughts become your words.

Keep your WORDS POSITIVE
because your words become your behaviour.

Keep your BEHAVIOUR POSITIVE
because your behaviour becomes your habits.

Keep your HABITS POSITIVE
because your habits become your values.

Keep your VALUES POSITIVE
because your values become your destiny."

- Mahatma Gandhi

DON'T LIMIT YOURSELF
TAKE RISKS!

I learnt in my early 20s that the only way I could experience life in full colour was by taking chances and following what made my heart beat faster.

It was a big decision to leave the security of a well-paid job and embark on a new venture making leotards, but I just knew that I had to step outside of my comfort zone to follow my dreams or I could possibly regret it for the rest of my life.

A common misconception is that to believe in yourself you must be 100 per cent confident of success, and if you feel fear you must have doubts about your success. I don't believe this is necessarily true. If we feel fear, it doesn't mean we don't believe in ourselves, it just means that we know there could be some pain on our journey to success, but we are willing to step out of our comfort zone and experience that pain anyway.

In the early years of my business the risks were a lot smaller than they are today, but I think I had a lot less experience and confidence in myself, so they seemed life changing at the time.

I believe wherever you are in life, you should challenge yourself, because life is about overcoming obstacles and becoming better and stronger.

Mistakes aren't bad. The fear of mistakes though, will imprison you in your comfort zone and you will never move forward in life. Instead of being scared of making a mistake, be scared of not making one. Without mistakes there is no learning and no growth.

So when you are about to step out of your comfort zone, go out on a limb and follow you dreams, remember that all great discoveries and accomplishments were made by making mistake after mistake after mistake - first.

THEN GO OUT AND DO IT!

never give up

This is the catch-cry for Lorna Jane and definitely one of my all-time FAVOURITE personal mantras in life.

Having a NEVER GIVE UP attitude has helped me through some pretty tough times in life and I know it has done the same for so many of our staff and customers.

I was sitting in Brisbane Airport waiting to board a plane to Los Angeles in late 2012 when I received an email from one of my team members letting me know how Lorna Jane and the Never Give Up approach to living had changed her life forever.

Tanya had been working alongside my husband, Bill, at the Noosa Triathlon in 2010. During the hustle and excitement of the event, she received a phone call to say her Mum had been emergency airlifted to hospital and that cancer had hit for the third time in 12 years.

What she didn't know was that it was going to be the hardest fight of her Mum's life. She went into immediate lung surgery and when she woke up Tanya was there, waiting, straight from the triathlon in her Lorna Jane Never Give Up cap.

That cap became her Mum's icon and still is today. It hung on the top of her hospital bed, it was passed around the ward and - would you believe it - became the talking point of the nursing staff. That cap still sits on her bed and when tough times come around, Tanya and her Mum joke that she hasn't been wearing it nearly enough!

Tanya tells me, and I will quote her here:

"There is nothing more powerful to me than the core values of Lorna Jane. The beautiful husband and wife team have taught me how to grow. Never look back, move forward, stand tall, don't waste time, love what you do every day, follow your dreams and never give up. They are only words but I live by them. Lorna Jane has provided me with tools to use in one of the hardest situations I expect I will ever face and my Mum has told me I am the one person she can rely on to bring positive energy to every situation we face on this roller coaster journey of her illness. The two women who inspire me the most: my Mum for her courage and determination, and my mentor Lorna Jane Clarkson, who on all counts has taught me to Never Give Up and to live your dream every day."

When I read Tanya's message I was overwhelmed with emotion that she had to face such challenges but equally grateful that Bill and I could help in such a small, but to Tanya, significant way.

I guess what this has taught me is that you really can never be sure of how having a Never Give Up attitude, and wanting to make a positive difference in people's lives, can actually play out.

Having a Never Give Up attitude can help you through darker times in your life, but it can also lead to great success and I honestly question whether there is ever success without it?

The concept of persistence paying off and refusing to give up on your dreams is evident in this list of successful and inspiring people who were initially rejected by those around them, but believed in themselves enough to strive for greatness anyway:

STEVE JOBS ...

Was 30 when he was left devastated and depressed after being unceremoniously removed from the company he started. He went on to become one of the most visionary Americans of his generation – perhaps of all time - and the co-founder of Apple computer.

WALT DISNEY ...

Was fired from a newspaper for "lacking imagination" and "having no original thoughts." The creator of Mickey Mouse, founder of Disneyland, Disney World and the Disney motion picture megalith, had one of the most fertile imaginations the world has ever known.

OPRAH WINFREY ...

Was demoted from her job as a news anchor because she "wasn't fit for television." The American media titan and philanthropist became one of the world's most influential women with her self-titled TV talk show, the highest-rated program of its kind in history and which ran for 25 years.

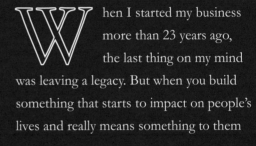

LEAVE A
LEGACY

When I started my business more than 23 years ago, the last thing on my mind was leaving a legacy. But when you build something that starts to impact on people's lives and really means something to them

- actually inspires them -

I think it's only natural that you want it to continue to impact people's lives once your time on this planet is over.

As pioneers of the Active Living Movement I feel it's absolutely paramount that Lorna Jane continues to grow, learn and inspire others. It's also important that we continue to innovate and be leaders in our category. Because it is only by striving to do this every single day, that we will be successful in keeping our message, products and brand aspirational to women all over the world.

Lorna Jane started out as a business that purely made active wear – I had always advocated a healthy life but had not for one minute imagined that it would cross over and become the brand philosophy and driving force in my life.

I still love designing active wear but I also really care about helping you achieve great things in your life and by doing this I get to feel significant – that I'm actually making a difference. I mean, what is the point of being alive if you don't at least try to do something remarkable? I want to make sure that Lorna Jane, Active Living and the Move Nourish Believe philosophy continues to inspire women to be fitter and healthier in their daily lives - forever!

Inspiring my team, our customers and women all over the world to be fitter and healthier and to achieve great things in their lives is more than just a job for me. It is my purpose, my cause, what I love to do and the reason I exist.

I want my time here to count for something. I want to continue to write books, to create new concepts so I can reach my customers on more levels - teach them about Active Living and be a resource for them to live longer, healthier and more fulfilled lives.

I will promote and inspire this abundant way of living till the day I die and hopefully what I achieve will continue long after I am gone.

WHAT
MOVES
Me

MOVE IT *or* LOSE IT

I work out on a daily basis wherever I am. It's a non-negotiable part of my day and vitally important part of my life because it clears my head, it's detoxifying, keeps me strong and means I don't have to worry about counting calories.

No matter how busy I get or how much pressure I am under, a workout makes me feel better. I come off the treadmill, out of the gym or off the yoga mat feeling relaxed and with a better sense of perspective about any challenges that lie ahead.

I also get many of my best ideas while I'm working out - ones that have actually changed the course of my life, and others as simple as deciding to change the position of a pocket on a pair of running shorts, or make the fabric softer for a yoga singlet.

But generally I just LOVE how regular exercise makes me feel: fit, healthy and positive. That's more than enough reason, as far as I'm concerned, to exercise every day for the rest of my life.

Many women hit the gym just to look better, but that can't be your only motivation otherwise chances are that you will feel discouraged and possibly give up if you don't see results fast enough. Regular exercise is about being healthy, and trust me you will feel healthier after your very first day!

You will find the sense of personal freedom that comes with regular exercise exhilarating. It's the foundation of positive brain chemistry, which burns more fat, boosts your immune system, improves your sleep and provides you with more overall zest for life.

And you'll have to agree, no one ever works out and regrets it! Because when you exercise daily and are in peak physical condition it positively influences every area of your life, helping you to think, perform and truly be at your best.

So why is it that so many women don't exercise? When the alternative is the likelihood of gaining weight, losing shape, risking health problems, having no energy, even being depressed, not to mention a general dissatisfaction with the way they look and feel.

the IMPORTANCE OF MOVING

In 2012 Lorna Jane commissioned Roy Morgan Research to collate statistics on Australians' attitudes to health and fitness to highlight our campaign to get the nation moving (for Active Nation Day).

Some of the findings were alarming to say the least:

while
11.7 million
AUSTRALIANS (63%) expressed a desire to **LOSE WEIGHT,** 53% did no formal **EXERCISE** in an average three-month period.

while
11.1 million
AUSTRALIANS said they **RESTRICT** HOW MUCH FATTENING FOOD THEY EAT, *about* 62% had visited a **FAST FOOD** outlet in the last 4 weeks.

nearly
7 million
AUSTRALIANS aged 18+ claim to be CONSTANTLY WATCHING **THEIR WEIGHT.** *However just* 29% of those actually had a BODY MASS INDEX in the healthy **WEIGHT RANGE.**

If these statistics have a message, it's that every one of us needs to reorganise and re-prioritise our lives so that we put our health first, and find the time to exercise on a regular basis.

Ironically, when you're so busy you could scream, taking time for physical activity couldn't be more important. Exercising gives you time to clear your mind and revitalise your body. It also boosts production of endorphins, our feel-good hormones, giving us a natural high.

As a result you will find you will live and work more efficiently, and what seemed like such a huge hassle before you went for that run, gym session or yoga class can be seen with a whole new, more positive perspective - a drop in the ocean that's easily overcome.

The hardest thing about exercising is to get started, but trust me, once you do get into a regular routine, you won't want to stop!

REGULAR EXERCISE WILL GIVE YOU *MORE* ...

energy

To help you run faster, dance longer and play harder.

flexibility

To keep you agile, youthful and feeling great.

bone and muscle strength

To allow you to do things with ease in your everyday life, such as enjoying long walks with your family, carrying your groceries up the stairs and generally being a more self-sufficient woman.

instant therapy

To help alleviate the stresses of your day, leaving you calm and peaceful but with increased energy.

quality sleep

It will help you fall asleep more easily and wake up more refreshed.

ability to manage your weight

Eating just 500 calories more than your body can use as energy per day translates into a weight gain of around half a kilo a week, or 2kg a month. So move it and burn those extra calories!

muscle tone

Even if you don't gain weight, lack of muscle tone will make you look larger and out of shape.

self-esteem

Gaining weight makes many people feel self-conscious to the point that they avoid socialising and comfort themselves by eating even more.

EXERCISE RITUALS TO FIT YOUR LIFE

Before I had my own business there was so much MORE time I could devote to exercise. And, of course, I taught fitness classes, so I exercised on the job!

But as my business grew and the time commitment increased, I found it more and more challenging to schedule exercise into my day.

Like most people, I let it slip for a little while and was just content to find a couple of hours to work out on the weekends.

However, I soon found that my energy levels weren't what they had been and I generally didn't feel as good about myself.

So I started getting up a little earlier every morning to work out and I can honestly say I have never looked back.

My morning workouts are now something I look forward to; they give me time to think and plan my day and they have become something that I would find hard to live without.

Some days, when my schedule is particularly busy or I have to make an early morning flight, I might only get in a 30-minute workout, but I do it anyway because it has become part of my DNA, and I don't feel the same if I skip it.

Over time I have come up with some great 15, 20 and 30-minute workouts that I will outline for you to try. I think you will find that they are definitely worth doing and highly effective if you put in 100 per cent effort.

DO ANYWHERE **LEG WORKOUT**

20 SQUATS	50 SEC WALL SQUATS
30 LUNGES	40 SUMO SQUATS
40 CALF RAISES	30 LEG RAISES
50 SEC WALL SQUAT	20 SQUATS
100 JUMPING JACKS	AND REPEAT.

HOTEL ROOM WORKOUT

60 SEC PLANK	30 SQUATS
50 CRUNCHES	20 TRICEP DIPS
40 BICYCLE CRUNCHES	10 PUSH-UPS
60 SEC WALL SIT	

REPEAT
UNTIL YOU
FEEL GOOD!

CARDIO CRUNCHDOWN

2 MIN WALK
10 MIN RUN
1 MIN WALK
1 MIN SPRINT

REPEAT
5 TIMES

60 CRUNCHES
1 MIN WALL SIT
1 MIN PLANK
5 MIN STRETCH

---

1 MIN PLANK
15 BICYCLE CRUNCHES
30-SEC SIDE PLANK (RIGHT SIDE)
15 BICYCLE CRUNCHES

30 SEC SIDE PLANK (LEFT SIDE)
15 REVERSE CRUNCHES
1 MIN V-SIT
3 MIN REST

AB-TASTIC WORKOUT

REPEAT
3 TIMES!

when 30 minutes is IMPOSSIBLE TO FIND

I have already talked to you about what exercise I do on a regular basis but one of the other important things about Active Living is that you make a conscious effort to move more on a regular basis in your everyday life.

So for those days when you are finding it absolutely impossible to block out an hour, or half an hour to work out, don't despair because I'm here to tell you that you can still increase your heart rate and burn off some of those extra kilos by incorporating small amounts of exercise into your everyday life. It's called 'incidental exercise' and it's a great way to get fit and burn some extra calories without noticing. All you need to do is find a few extra minutes here and there. After all, even a small amount of exercise is better than none at all.

For me, incidental exercise includes things like walking my dog, which I do twice a day, taking the stairs, walking to the local store instead of hopping in the car, and running my own errands at work instead of asking one of my staff to do them for me.

TURN A GET-TOGETHER INTO AN EXERCISE OPPORTUNITY.

You're off to meet someone for lunch or coffee. Why not meet and go for a walk first? It's amazing how enjoyable exercise can be combined with a little stimulating conversation and the company of a good friend. Make it a regular date; you'll be helping a friend get fit and there's always that cappuccino waiting for you when you finish, for a little added motivation.

WALK MORE.

Take a walk in your lunch break, or walk your dog on the weekends. It's a great way to clear your head, get some fresh air and escape the house or office. Another good idea is to walk your kids to school. As well as being good for your health and the health of your children, time spent without the distractions of TV, homework and computer games will do wonders for your relationships.

DO TWO THINGS AT ONCE.

Learn to look at every activity as a chance to exercise your body. Dance a little while you dust; do leg-lifts or knee bends while you're brushing your teeth. When you're on your mobile do some stretching or walk around the room, you could even do some pelvic floor exercises while you're making dinner or watching television. Have some fun with it and use your imagination. The only rule is to keep moving.

PLAY WITH YOUR KIDS.

Instead of using the excuse that you can't exercise because you're looking after the kids, why not get outside and join them? Turn off the TV and play cricket, go bike riding or have a go on the swings. You'll have a whole lot of fun too.

TURN SHOPPING INTO A WORKOUT.

I was telling everyone prior to Christmas that shopping was my cardio! So why not stick to that mindset and get a mini workout while picking up a few of your favourite things? Park a little further away than usual from the shops and walk further. Take the stairs instead of the lift and if you use the escalator, use it as a Stair Master and get those legs moving to improve your cardiovascular system and tone your buttocks and thighs. Lastly, resist the temptation to put everything in a trolley. Carry your shopping and use the weight of the bags as muscle-toning resistance on your way back to the car.

"SHOPPING IS MY CARDIO."
- Carrie Bradshaw

Incidental exercise is a perfect example to show that by simply changing your mindset you can easily find ways to move a little more on those days when you just can't find that 30 minutes or full hour of dedicated workout time.

So give it a go; there is no time like the present to make incidental exercise a part of your day, every day, and feel the difference.

#LJINCIDENTALEXERCISE

THE POWER OF
STRENTH TRAINING

I must confess that I was a late convert to the world of strength training. I thought that cardio was the answer to keeping myself fit and in shape and that lifting weights was just for boys.

I had dabbled a little with some Body Pump classes, New Body classes and some circuit training but any muscle I gained was quickly burnt off by all the daily running and aerobic exercise I was doing at the same time.

Like so many women, I didn't realise the positive impact of strength training and the many benefits it could bring to my life as well as my body.

When you introduce it into your exercise routine you will see and feel the difference quickly by losing weight, gaining muscle and toning and sculpting your body the way you have always wanted.

THESE ARE SOME OF THE MAJOR BENEFITS OF STRENGTH TRAINING:

YOU WILL LOSE BODY FAT
The more lean muscle your body has, the more calories it burns.

YOU WILL BE PHYSICALLY STRONGER
Through weight training you can expect a substantial increase in your strength so everyday activities will become easier, from carrying the groceries to climbing stairs and lifting heavy objects.

YOU WILL HELP PREVENT INJURY
The stronger we are the less chance of injury, because lifting weights strengthens your muscles and tendons. This is especially important as we get older because strengthening muscles around our joints is one of the best ways to prevent and recover from injury.

YOU WILL REDUCE HEALTH RISKS
Weight training can improve the way the body processes sugar, which lessens your risk of diabetes.

YOU WILL LOOK MORE TONED
Strength training will improve your physical appearance by adding lean muscle more effectively than any other form of exercise.

Regular strength training has made me physically stronger in my 40s than I ever was in my 20s and 30s. It has also improved my posture and I honestly feel I am in the best shape of my life!
AND ONE OF THE BIGGEST SURPRISES OF ALL

— I ACTUALLY LOVE IT!

FIT FACTS

Lifting heavier weights for fewer reps burns more fat than lighter weights and more reps.

◇◇◇◇◇◇◇◇◇◇◇◇◇◇◇◇◇

A shorter workout at 75% *of your aerobic capacity will give your metabolism a bigger boost than sweating longer at* 50%.

Women who don't eat for long periods are more likely to have higher body-fat percentages than women who eat more regularly.

Alternating bouts of high and low intensity cardio has been shown to have more fat-burning benefits than going at a consistent pace (even if your consistent pace is running or cycling like the wind!).

Doing slow versus normal speed reps with free weights (including hand weights) increases muscle strength by about 50%. More muscle = metabolism boost = higher rate of fat burning. Using free weights also activates more muscle fibres than using machines.

Between birth and old age, you will walk about 113,000km. Walking is one of the best activities you can do to keep your heart-lung complex in good working condition.

500g of muscle burns about 9 calories a day. 500g of fat only burns 2 calories.

Don't eat a big meal close to bedtime. Your metabolism is slower while you sleep so your body won't digest food and burn fat as efficiently as during the day.

EATING A PROTEIN-PACKED BREAKFAST and lunch helps you burn more post-meal fat than if you eat lower-protein meals. For instance, two eggs for breakfast will help you trim more weight and body fat than if you ate the same amount of kilojoules in a bagel.

◇◇◇◇◇◇◇◇◇◇◇◇◇◇◇◇◇

Listening to up-tempo music has been proven to make you run faster and harder than classical and other slower-paced music.

Going harder during the first half of your workout and taking it easier during the second burns up to 23% more fat than doing it the other way around.

The human body has more than 650 muscles. If every muscle worked together at the same time, you could lift about 680kg.

◇◇◇◇◇◇◇◇◇◇◇◇◇◇◇◇◇◇◇◇◇◇◇◇◇◇◇◇◇◇

Visualising a specific exercise actually causes the muscle synapses to fire as if you were doing it. Unfortunately, this doesn't mean you can just get fit through mind power, but it can really psych you up for a more effective workout.

KEEPING A FOOD DIARY can help you manage your weight. When you force yourself to write down every single thing you eat and drink, you may be unpleasantly surprised to see some of the choices you are making and how much more you may be eating than you realise.

Running puts 4 to 7 times your body weight in pressure on your feet. So make sure you invest in good quality, comfortable, well-fitted running shoes.

In order to burn off a fast food chain big burger (about 550 calories), a 63kg woman would have to run for 52 minutes at a 10 minutes/1.6km pace.

The more you exercise, the more your body learns to burn fat rather than storing it.

Stress raises levels of the steroid hormone cortisol, which can drive you to eat more. It is also believed to create a tendency to accumulate more fat on the abdomen than other areas of the body.

◇◇◇◇◇◇◇◇◇◇◇◇◇◇◇◇◇◇◇◇◇◇◇◇◇◇◇◇◇◇

People who run for at least 4 hours a week use up more calories than non-runners, even when they're not running.

YOU'RE NEVER TOO OLD TO EXERCISE.

According to Running USA, runners 50 years and older represent one of the fastest-growing age groups participating in marathons. As the total number of runners finishing marathons in the US doubled to 518,000 in the 20 years ending 2011, the number of finishers aged 50-plus nearly tripled to 92,200, or about 18 per cent of the total. More than 1 in 5 finishers at the 2011 New York Marathon, or 9,710 athletes, ran in 50-and-older age groups.

There is no "best time" to exercise that applies to all people. The best time is when it works for you.

DRESS THE PART

Over 23 years ago I was motivated to start designing my own active wear because I was disappointed in the choices that were available and just wanted to wear something that made me look and feel good when I worked out.

Over time, the culture of Lorna Jane and the core values around how we design and innovate our products has essentially remained the same – we want you to be motivated to exercise, we want you to look fashionably fit and we want our products to out-perform the toughest of your workouts, but we also want you to be comfortable enough that you want to wear them in your everyday life.

I have developed a routine of laying my active wear out each night in anticipation of my morning workout. It makes for one less thing I have to do in the morning but more importantly, makes me look forward to my run or yoga class just by applying a little ceremony similar to that of deciding what you are going to wear for a special occasion.

Here are some of my favourite outfits for the different exercise I do, to give you some ideas and inspire you for your next workout:

#favoutfitlornajane

the *YOGA outfit*

For me what I wear to yoga has to be about comfort - so give me a fold-over waist and loose fitting singlet teamed with a supportive crop and I am ready to go!

the CARDIO outfit

I do most of my cardio outside, so layering and a visor are mandatory - so is having a maximum support sports bra and a pocket to stash my keys and ipod.

the STRENGTH outfit

Core Support is key for strength training - so I like to wear a high-waisted tight (usually with core compression), a cute crop top and a looser cut-away singlet - so I can see my muscles working!

FUEL YOUR BODY

Nutrition is the foundation of our health. That's why it's important to think about what we put into our mouths every time we eat or drink, and ask ourselves the question - will this have a positive or negative effect on my body?

Proper nutrition is equally important for athletic performance, so think of the foods you eat as 'fuel' and what you choose to eat before and after you exercise as having a significant impact on your performance and recovery.

What you eat, how much and how close before or after can be an individual thing, so my advice is to try different foods over time, and for your different workouts, to see what works best for you.

The basic rules to follow are that pre-workout snacks should be a combination of protein and complex carbohydrates with some fat. They also need to be light enough that they don't weigh you down or make you feel sluggish and convenient enough that you will actually eat them! Some of my go-to pre-workout snacks can be as simple as a banana, a boiled egg with a piece of fruit or a bowl of oatmeal.

For maximum benefit, post-workout snacks need to be consumed within 30 minutes of your workout and should include at least 30g of protein and some carbohydrates - whilst keeping the fat content low. Post-workout snacks keep your metabolism burning, improve strength and keep you from feeling light-headed or dizzy.

Some of my quick and easy post-workout staples are: a handful of almonds with a fresh juice, vegetable sticks with homemade hummus or something as simple as a chocolate protein shake made with water or coconut water.

It is equally important that you are well hydrated before, during and after you exercise. And if you are doing lots of high-intensity exercise, electrolytes such as sodium, potassium, chloride and magnesium must be replaced as they play a major role in restoring water balance within your body.

Sports drinks are commonly used to restore electrolyte balance but I don't like to recommend them as they can include high amounts of refined sugar, artificial flavours, colours and other additives that don't really shout 'Good Health' to me!

I recommend coconut water as a good, natural and totally delicious option to replenish electrolytes, but be sure to stay away from any tricked-up variations and stick to natural, unsweetened brands only.

açai bowl

Makes 2 serves
Prep time: 5 mins

2 sachets 100%
pureed açai berries
1 large banana,
frozen
1 cup frozen berries
(of choice)

¼-½ cup coconut
water, depending on
desired consistency
Toppings: spiced nuts,
granola, fresh berries
or banana

*Place all ingredients into a food processor.
Blend until smooth. Serve with toppings.
Best eaten immediately, but can be stored
in an airtight container in the freezer.*

egg sandwich

Makes 2 serves
Prep time: 15 mins
Cook time: 10 mins

2 sheets nori
4 eggs,
boiled & peeled
salt & pepper to taste
1 avocado
¼ capsicum, julienned

1 medium carrot,
julienned
50g snowpea sprouts
(or any other sprout
variety)

*Using a fork, mash the boiled eggs, salt
and pepper. Place both sheets of nori on
a flat surface, and spread ½ of the egg
mix onto each sheet. Layer the avocado,
sprouts and thinly sliced veggies on one
of the nori sheets. Place the other nori
sheet on top with the egg facing down.*

quinoa fruit salad

Makes 4 serves
Prep time: 5 mins
Cook time: 20 mins

1 cup cooked quinoa
1/3 cup raspberries
1/3 cup blueberries
1 nectarine, chopped
1/2 cup red grapes

½ cup green grapes
1 punnet strawberries,
quartered
2 tbsp mint leaves,
chopped

*In a large bowl, place all ingredients
and mix well to incorporate. Change fruit
according to personal preference
or season.*

poached
chicken
WITH
& PESTO
CRACKERS

crackers

2 cups wholemeal
spelt flour
¼ cup extra virgin olive oil

2 tsp sea salt
2 tsp pepper

Makes 4 serves
Prep time: 30 mins
Cook time: 40 mins

Spinach crackers add:
2 cups spinach,
blended until smooth
in food processor with
2 tbsp water and 2 tsp
lemon juice.

Beetroot crackers add:
2 tbsp grated beetroot,
blended until smooth in
food processor with
2 tbsp water.

poached chicken

chicken breasts, 1
breast per serve
1L room temp. water
whole white
peppercorns
peel of 1 large orange

knob of ginger
1 spanish onion,
cut into quarters
2 star anise (optional)

In a large pot, place all of the ingredients.

Cover with a lid, and bring up to a boil. When it boils, turn the heat down to a slow simmer. Simmer for 10 mins.

After 10 mins, take off the heat, but keep the chicken covered in the pot for a further 10 mins. Check to see if chicken is cooked, then remove from water.

pesto

½ large bunch
silverbeet,
destemmed
1 cup walnuts,
roasted
1 clove garlic, peeled

3 tbsp extra virgin
olive oil
½ lemon, juice
½ cup basil leaves
1 tsp sea salt
½ tsp pepper

Combine all ingredients into a food processor, and blend until smooth.

Taste to see if needs more seasoning or lemon juice.

Combine all cracker ingredients into bowl using your hands. Divide dough in two, and place into two separate bowls. Add spinach paste to one bowl, and the beetroot paste to the other. Keeping the mix in the bowl, use floured hands to gently knead the vegetables into the cracker mix.

It should form a sticky dough.

Preheat oven to 180°C.

Place each ball of dough onto baking paper. Flatten slightly, placing another piece of baking paper on top. Using a rolling pin flatten the dough until it is approximately ½ cm thick. Take off the top layer of baking paper, and lift the dough onto a baking tray using the bottom sheet of baking paper.

Using a knife or pizza cutter, lightly cut the dough into shapes resembling your desired cracker size and shape. Place in the oven and cook for 20 mins.

Break along the cuts when cooled. Store in the freezer in an airtight container.

recovery
drink

Makes 2 serves
Prep time: 5 mins

½ lemon, juice & zest
½ lime, juice
3 medjool dates, pitted
1 tbsp honey
1 tbsp vanilla flavoured protein powder
1 tsp wakame or dulse
1 tbsp coconut oil
½ tsp maca powder
2 cups water

Put all ingredients into a food processor
and blend until smooth. Serve with ice.

NB: do not be discouraged by the sea
vegetable, they do not impart a strong
flavour in this drink; if you do not have
any, however, substitute with coconut
water instead of water.

Share your
pre & post
workout snacks
on instagram
#MNBfuelright

apple & peanut butter
stacks

Makes 2 serves
Prep time: 10 mins

2 green apples
¼ cup peanut butter
dried blueberries

Slice apples into thick sections,
widthwise, removing any seeds.

Spread peanut butter liberally over the top
of each apple slice, except the slice from
the top of the apple. Sprinkle each slice
with a few dried blueberries.

Layer slices on top of each other,
leaving the top of the apple for last.

yoghurt

& spiced nuts

Makes 2 serves
Prep time: 5 mins

1 cup unsweetened,
natural yoghurt
½ cup spiced nuts

spiced nuts

3 cups nuts: mixture of almonds,
cashews, macadamias, walnuts,
Brazil, pecans
1 cup seeds: mixture of
sunflower, chia and pepitas
(do not use flaxseed or hemp
seeds as the fats are too volatile
for the cooking process)
2 tbsp honey
3-4tsp cinnamon, ground
2 tsp nutmeg, ground
1 tsp cardamom, ground
1 tsp ginger, ground

Preheat oven to 150°C.

*Mix nuts, seeds and spices
together in a bowl.*

*Drizzle honey over and toss a
few times to coat the nuts and
seeds. Spread nuts over a lined
baking tray and cook in the
150°C oven for 10 mins.*

*Stir well, and then cook again
for another 5 mins.*

energy bars

Makes 12 serves
Prep time: 30 mins

2 cups macadamias, shelled
1 cup raw unsalted cashews
1 cup rolled oats
1 ½ cups medjool dates
(approx. 16), pitted
1 tbsp vanilla paste
½ tsp sea salt
½ cup dessicated coconut
1-2 tbsp coconut oil
(if required)

toppings

goji berries & hazelnuts
coconut flakes & dried blueberries
pepitas & cacao nibs

*Soak the dates in a bowl of
water for 15-20 mins, and
then drain.*

*In a food processor blend the
macadamias, cashews and
oats into a fine crumb.*

*Add the rest of the ingredients
and blend until mix can be
pressed into a ball in your
hand. If too dry, add some
coconut oil 1 tbsp at a time.*

*Very firmly press the mix onto
a lined baking tray with the
palms of your hands.*

*Set in the freezer for
10-15 mins, or until firm.*

*Press desired toppings into the
energy bars.*

*Return to freezer to harden
and then portion into 12
individual bars.*

Best stored in freezer.

EATING
FOR LIFE

finding the right food balance

With so many conflicting messages out there about food, what we should eat, and what we shouldn't, you can't help but get a little confused about what is the best thing you can do, and I guess how you should nourish your body to be healthy and in tip-top condition.
We know we need to eat fresh and nutritious ingredients; that we should eat often, avoid sugar and overly processed foods and drink loads and loads of water. But every day there seems to be a new health food, miracle ingredient, or anti-ageing and anti-cancerous breakthrough that gets us wondering whether we should try it just in case.

I think it's a good idea to have an open mind and stay up-to-date with new ideas but more importantly, remember to put your health first, do your own research and ultimately stick to what works for YOU.

I don't have the perfect body, and like most women I have things I want to improve, but I have learnt to do the best with what I have. I'm fit and healthy, but I also enjoy eating a little dessert now and again, cappuccinos with my friends and the occasional cocktail to celebrate a special occasion. I don't indulge in these foods on a daily basis but it's nice to know that I can have them now and again when I really feel like it.

That's where the 80/20 APPROACH to eating comes in. I find by eating healthy and nutritious food 80 per cent of the time I am putting my health first, and then when I want to indulge in a little of what I love (the other 20 per cent) I don't feel guilty about doing it.

LIFE SHOULDN'T BE ABOUT DEPRIVING YOURSELF, SO MY ADVICE IS TO CONCENTRATE ON BEING HEALTHY.

If you want some ice-cream, have some ice-cream, just don't eat the whole tub or have it after every meal.

The 80/20 rule is what I live by every day. It represents my commitment to live a full and long life in absolute best health. I have made it my goal to eat for vitality, good health and to always give my body the nutrients it needs, to say "NO" to dieting and to look after my whole self.

This means eating well every day so you are never tempted to take on fad diets, drastic detox programs and liquid cleanses. Be healthy most of the time, indulge yourself a little, and remember the most important thing is to find the food balance that works for YOU. Don't deprive yourself of the things you love; and never, never, never forget that food is meant to be nourishing your body, but also to be celebrated and enjoyed.

Another thing to remember is that you can only eat what you make available — so if you only have good food in your fridge then that is all you will want to eat.

KEEP IT CLEAN

I hear women talking about how they watch their diet and exercise regularly but frequently feel tired, sluggish, and bloated. Their skin is dry and dull and they can't budge those extra kilos and don't understand why.

I can guarantee it has everything to do with what they're eating, or not eating, because what you feed your body affects how you look as well as everything you think, feel and do.

Good nutrition, digestion and an efficient metabolism are essential for your mind and body to be in peak condition and to maintain your ideal weight. So what do you imagine is happening if you're consuming pre-packaged, highly processed or refined foods containing preservatives, artificial colours and flavours, high in 'trans' fats, sugar and salt, and have possibly been in frozen storage for months before sale?

Sadly, many people may not even know their diet is unhealthy. They are buying foods they believe are good for them but actually contain hidden nasties like those I've mentioned.

This is where clean eating comes in, and you'll be hearing a lot more about it. It's not a diet or health fad, but a sustainable, wonderful way of life that works really well within the realms of the 80/20 approach to eating. It's eating food in its most natural state - I guess you'd call it eating real food, the way nature intended.

Its purpose is not weight loss, but it's highly likely you will drop kilos when your body isn't overloaded dealing with chemicals.

Most of you have probably heard of clean eating, but are possibly not sure how CLEAN clean eating really has to be?

Clean eating stems from the idea of eliminating, or reducing, chemicals from the body - that means removing as many packaged and processed products from your diet as possible.

Clean eating is basically eating only, whole fresh foods that consist of lean meats, good carbs, loads of vegetables, fruit and salad and good fats. Basically, any foods that you could catch, pick or gather.

I don't follow a strict eating plan as I mentioned in the 80/20 section, but have been eating clean for quite a few years now. It makes me feel good that I am eating foods that are as close to their natural state as possible and allows me to focus on nourishing my body so that I always feel full of energy and ready for anything life throws at me.

I also make sure that I eat smaller meals regularly (5-6 times a day). This stops me reaching for fast and convenient snack foods but also keeps my metabolism working well and burns more fat. Eating smaller meals more often also puts less pressure on my digestive system which keeps my blood sugar levels balanced and keeps my energy levels high.

CLEAN FOODS

Clean foods contain very few ingredients and include fresh fruit and vegetables, complex carbohydrates (whole grains such as millet, oats, wheat germ, barley, wild rice, brown rice, buckwheat, oat bran; also fruit, vegetables and legumes) and lean proteins, which include:

FISH. ONE OF THE BEST SOURCES OF LEAN PROTEIN, lower in saturated fat than meats. Excellent choices are cold water fish like salmon, that have high levels of omega-3 fatty acids, a good fat that promotes good health from head to toe.

CHICKEN, TURKEY AND LEAN BEEF. Be sure to trim off any fat before cooking and when shopping for minced beef, choose lean or extra lean.

EGGS HAVE BEEN GIVEN A BAD RAP IN THE PAST as being a villain aggravating your cholesterol levels but they provide an astounding 5g of protein per serve. They are also a cheap source of protein, from a simple boiled egg for an energy hit - to making omelettes, quiches or frittatas. I recommend you eat your eggs whole because that is how nature intended it, and if you are worried about your cholesterol just eat a smaller quantity.

BEANS, PEAS AND LENTILS (LEGUMES) ARE DELICIOUS, fibre-rich and filling proteins that can be eaten alone or in soups, salads, casseroles and rissoles. Ideal for vegetarians. Start with small serves and work up to what your body is comfortable with, as consuming too much fibre can cause bloating, flatulence and even cramps.

> *A GOOD GUIDE WHEN CHOOSING CLEAN FOODS IS TO AVOID ANY PRODUCT WITH A LONG INGREDIENT LIST AS THIS IS A CLEAR INDICATION THAT IT IS MAN-MADE AND NOT CONSIDERED 'CLEAN'.*

ALSO ON THE DUBIOUS LIST are mass-produced breads, pastas, white rice, white flour and foods containing any of these on their list of ingredients. Other foods to avoid are anything high in saturated and trans fats, fried or high in sugar.

BECOME USED TO READING LABELS ON TINNED AND PACKAGED FOODS. If they contain more than six ingredients, it's safe to say they're not healthy. If you can't understand what an ingredient is, even more reason not to buy the product.

This may sound challenging if you haven't heard of, or considered clean eating before. But you don't have to turn your life upside down on day one.

TAKE SMALL STEPS; MAKE SMALL CHANGES EVERY DAY until you have effectively swapped all of your processed foods with clean alternatives.

For example, start making your own juice rather than buying it in a carton, buy coffee beans and grind them yourself rather than drinking instant coffee, and maybe even start your own herb or veggie garden.

Lastly, if you are used to a diet of mostly processed foods, you might find eating clean a little bland for the first week or two. BUT RESIST THE URGE TO ADD SUGAR AND SALT because I assure you, after just a little time, your taste buds will adapt and you will appreciate just how delicious clean food can be.

BUYING ORGANIC

We've talked about the 80/20 rule and eating clean, so now the last thing on the list to consider for maximum good health is 'buying organic'.

This means eating the way our grandparents or great-grandparents would have — that is meat, poultry, fruit, grains and vegetables grown without added hormones, antibiotics, or pesticides.

There is now plentiful research showing that organic food — fruits, vegetables and grains — are far superior in vitamin, mineral and nutrient content, while at the same time being much lower, or having no harmful herbicides, fungicides, pesticides or artificial fertiliser chemicals that can be present in non-organic produce.

To be labelled organic, organic food production must be free of antibiotics, anti-microbials, hormones and other growth promotants. Similarly, the processing of organic food must be free from the use of synthetic chemicals such as preservatives, colourings, and antioxidants. Meats, dairy and eggs organically produced are without antibiotics, growth hormones or genetically modified vaccines.

Organic agriculture also feeds the earth, not just you! Whilst not all organic farms are the same, most replace key elements back into the soil naturally. Industrial farming, on the other hand, leaches nutrients from the soil and so more and more fertilisers and other additives are needed every year.

So the great thing, and what I personally love about buying organic, is that you can be sure that your food is as close to natural and chemical-free as possible, which in today's modern (and sadly often toxic) world has to be good!

While it's best to buy organic, sometimes organic food isn't available, or it's just out of our price range, so if you have to pick and choose what to buy organically, or find yourself in a place where it just isn't an available option, here are some lists of the most and least contaminated foods to use as your buying guide. ❯ ❯

THE DIRTY DOZEN

- the 12 MOST CONTAMINATED when industrially farmed:

1. APPLES	2. GRAPES	3. RASPBERRIES
4. CAPSICUMS	5. NECTARINES	6. POTATOES
7. CELERY	8. PEACHES	9. SPINACH
10. CHERRIES	11. PEARS	12. STRAWBERRIES

THE CLEAN DOZEN

- the 12 LEAST-CONTAMINATED fruit and vegetables are:

1. ASPARAGUS	2. SWEET CORN	3. PEAS
4. AVOCADOS	5. PAPAYAS	6. BROCCOLI
7. CAULIFLOWER	8. BANANAS	9. MANGOES
10. ONIONS	11. KIWI FRUIT	12. PINEAPPLES

another important thing to remember:

when you're buying both organic and non-organic produce always wash your fruit and vegetables prior to cooking or eating, to make sure first that it is clean and then to reduce any pesticide residues.

FOOD
rituals

Like most things in life, when you find a good thing you should stick to it, and that's how I feel about eating. You can try lots of different things in the pursuit of health and vitality, some that you do for a while, and others that you want to do for the rest of your life.

But once you have found what works for you, my advice is to stick to it for as long as it makes you feel good, while always being open to trying new things.

HERE ARE SOME OF MY BASIC FOOD RITUALS THAT I PRACTISE EVERY DAY AND HAVE BECOME THE FOUNDATION OF MY HEALTH AND WELLBEING:

I drink a glass of WARM WATER and lemon juice first thing in the morning to kick-start my metabolism, balance my PH and detox my body.

As far as food is concerned I make sure I am PREPARED and always have some snacks on-hand whether it be at work, at home or when I'm out and about in general. I pack containers of nuts, protein powder and a couple of pieces of fruit with me at all times - oh, and plenty of water!

I drink at least TWO TO THREE LITRES of pure water throughout the day, every day. I find that if I become even just a little dehydrated, my body becomes tired and sluggish. I also find that if for some reason I don't get my daily dose of water, my skin starts to look less radiant and healthy.

I love JUICES AND SMOOTHIES and have at least one to two every day. Each glass is a power-packed, delicious meal, and so quick and easy to make. Sometimes I will have two smoothies in the morning (one for breakfast and one as a mid-morning snack), other days I have a more substantial breakfast and keep my juices or smoothies for mid-morning and afternoon snacks.

I always eat a healthy BREAKFAST. It literally 'breaks my fast' after the night's sleep and if I'm completely honest, I find I can't function properly without it. Breakfast starts my inner motor, gives me energy and puts me in a good mood for the rest of the day.

I limit myself to ONE COFFEE a day, and try not to have any caffeine after lunch. I do this to make sure I can relax and unwind towards the end of the day and sleep well through the night.

For as long as I can remember I have had DESSERT after my evening meal. It doesn't have to be anything crazy and sometimes it's simply a couple of squares of dark chocolate or a single scoop of my homemade banana ice-cream - but I always finish my day with a celebration of something sweet.

goodness
IN A GLASS

No chapter on healthy eating would be complete without a comprehensive discussion on juicing and smoothies — which and I must admit are two of my favourite things.

I am often asked what is my preference between juicing and making fruit and veggie-based drinks with a blender and I honestly think both are amazing additions to any diet.

Juice allows us to work with the freshest fruits, vegetables and herbs to create drinks that are deliciously vibrant, deliver an amazing nutritional punch and are incredibly easy to digest. But smoothies have their place on my daily menu as well because they offer fibre, good fats and opportunities for adding protein into your diet all while tasting deliciously decadent.

One of the greatest benefits of juicing is that it gives you an incredible amount of vitamins and minerals in one hit. And when most of us don't have enough fresh vegetables on a daily basis, juicing is a sure way to add those necessary nutrients back into your diet. It's also good for anyone with digestive issues, as the pulp and fibre is removed, enabling nutrients to be easily absorbed across the intestinal wall.

Green juices also have an anti-inflammatory effect that can calm an upset stomach and boost immune function.

The downside to juicing is that all too often we consume too much sugar in the process. So a good rule of thumb is to never juice more fruit or vegetables than you would eat in one sitting.

I often see people drinking huge juices that would contain up to four or five carrots, an apple and half a head of celery. Not only is the sugar content too high, but you most definitely wouldn't be able to sit down and consume that in its original form on a plate in one sitting.

- You don't need to rush out and buy a juicer. Visiting a local health food store that makes organic fresh juices is a good way to start. They will have perfected the quantities and combinations and cost-wise it works out to be the same.

- Whether you make it at home or buy it, it is best to drink your juice straight away as it is highly perishable. If you want to get the most out of your juice, use a cold pressed masticating juicer instead of a centrifugal juicer. You will get more nutrients and your juice will last for three days in an airtight container in the fridge.

- Try other enhancers to make your juices delicious: things like lemons, ginger or shredded coconut. Not only will the coconut taste delicious, but the coconut fat will help your body absorb the fat-soluble vitamins in your juice.

I am a total fan of smoothies because they are so easy to make, you can throw both fresh and frozen produce in, and the clean-up is minimal. You can also make up a big batch (like I do with my Super Green Smoothie) and it will last in portioned airtight containers for up to three days without losing any of its nutrients (add a little lemon juice if you want it to keep its green colour).

When you drink smoothies your body benefits from the phytonutrients found in the skin and flesh of the fruit and veggies. You also benefit from the large amounts of fibre found in whole fruit and vegetables that is important for regulating blood sugar, keeping your bowels regular, helping with hunger control and maybe even preventing certain types of cancer.

MY TOP TIPS FOR SMOOTHIES ARE:

- Simply load up your blender with fresh or frozen fruits, green leafy vegetables, and liquid such as coconut water, juice or almond milk. You can also add a superfood kick or supplement to your smoothie like Acai, Spirulina or Maca Powder. Just toss in a teaspoon for an extra boost of whatever you need.

- Buy organic if you are using the whole fruit or vegetable to avoid any contamination from the skin.

- Add ice if you want it super cold or thicker in texture.

Smoothie blends and juicing are different: Both boost immunity and stimulate repair and renewal of cells. However, if you are looking for a hit of energy, vitamins and minerals and don't care about the calories then juices are a good option. If you want a more balanced food source or meal, and are watching your calorie intake, and need a little more fibre in your diet, then Smoothies are the better option for you.

Here are two of my favourite Smoothie recipes for you to try:

My fav Smoothie RECIPES

green smoothie

Makes 1-2 serves
Prep time: 5 mins

3 cups spinach
1 inch knob of ginger
1 orange

1 small banana
½ pear
2 cups water

Chop all ingredients into similar size pieces, removing any skin, cores or seeds. Place all ingredients into a high powered blender, and blend on high until completely smooth.

Drink immediately, or store in a tightly sealed glass jar in the fridge for up to 3 days.

This recipe would be more of a light meal or snack recipe as it contains high amounts of carbs/fruit.

meal replacement smoothie

Makes 1 serve
Prep time: 35 mins

1 banana,
peeled and chopped
½ cup frozen berries
2 tbsp chia seeds

1 cup rice milk,
sugar-free
1 tsp coconut oil

Place all ingredients, except chia seeds, into a high powered blender.

Blend on high until smooth.

Add the chia seeds, and allow the smoothie to sit for at least half an hour for the chia seeds to gelatinise.

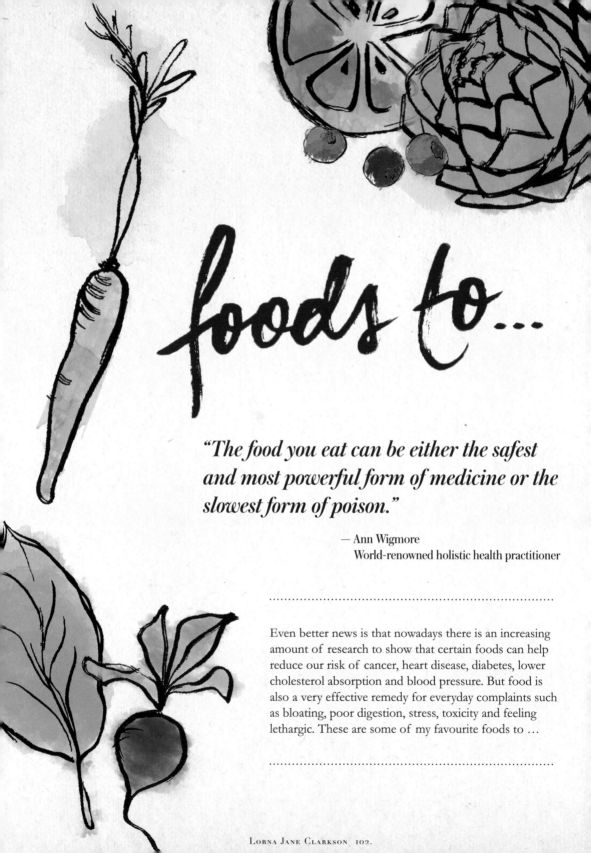

foods to...

"The food you eat can be either the safest and most powerful form of medicine or the slowest form of poison."

— Ann Wigmore
World-renowned holistic health practitioner

Even better news is that nowadays there is an increasing amount of research to show that certain foods can help reduce our risk of cancer, heart disease, diabetes, lower cholesterol absorption and blood pressure. But food is also a very effective remedy for everyday complaints such as bloating, poor digestion, stress, toxicity and feeling lethargic. These are some of my favourite foods to …

chill out

When life gets a little hectic, stay cool as a cucumber with these everyday foods that will calm your nerves and lift your spirits: Have a green salad or smoothie loaded with plenty of magnesium-rich spinach. Magnesium keeps our nerves and muscles relaxed, and is also a great source of vitamin A, C, iron and folate. Just another reason to have that square of dark chocolate after dinner – aside from all its heart-boosting antioxidants dark chocolate is rich in tryptophan which our bodies use to produce serotonin, a neuro-chemical that relaxes the brain and makes you sleep more soundly. Sip on a cup of green tea. Not only does it lower your risk of cardiovascular disease and cancer, reduce blood pressure and prevent hypertension and promote weight loss but it contains the amino acid L-theanine which reduces stress, promotes relaxation and enhances your mood.

beat bloating

No one likes to feel bloated and I've found the quickest and easiest way to reduce bloating is to take a small handful of mint leaves (mint teabags work too if you don't have the fresh stuff), a few slices of fresh ginger root and some lemon or orange slices and steep them in hot water for at least five minutes ... then sip. Ginger and mint are wonderful, natural bloat-fighters and the citrus adds vitamin C for extra yumminess and antioxidants for glowing skin. Another quick and easy option is to buy a bottle of peppermint essential oil (make sure it's food-grade) and take a few drops in water or straight onto your tongue after eating. This also acts as a great breath freshener.

detox

I believe that if you eat really well and reduce your intake or eliminate completely any toxin-laden foods from your diet, there really is no reason to feel you have to go on any form of regimented detox program or fast. It all starts by reducing the toxins in your system and that means eliminating or reducing your consumption of alcohol, caffeinated drinks, refined sugars, any highly processed or refined foods. Then there are many foods you should include in your diet every day that will help cleanse your liver, promote good liver and gallbladder function and stimulate healthy digestion.

Why not try these tips to cleanse and detoxify your system:

~ Citrus fruits are a great source of vitamin C, which is known to help the body detox and burn fat. Start the day by drinking water with lemon. I do this religiously every morning and find it to be refreshing, metabolism boosting and alkaline balancing.

~ Leafy greens eaten raw, in soups, juices or stir-fried, boost chlorophyll levels, stimulate your body's liver-cleansing enzymes and help rid the body of environmental toxins.

~ Eat beets to help the liver and gallbladder eliminate bile and other toxins.

~ Tumeric, ginger and garlic help the body get rid of free radicals and there are so many ways they can be used to add zest and taste to your food.

Fast foods are notorious anti-energy agents; high in bad fat, sugar, and salt. They are laden with empty calories and will zap your body of its energy producing B vitamins. So banish the chips and chocolate and fuel up instead with natural energy snacks such as:

~The perfectly packaged banana provides the same amount of energy as 'so-called' energy drinks but with more nutrients and zero artificial ingredients. They are also cheap, convenient, natural and contain antioxidants, with the additional boost of fibre, potassium and vitamin B6.

~ A Green Smoothie packs a huge amount of greens into one drink and is loaded with vitamins, enzymes, minerals, amino acids and filling fibre. It's perfect for breakfast or as a mid-afternoon snack when you feel low on energy.

~ Blueberries are a delicious and energy boosting snack and my absolute must-have treat when I go to the movies. These berries are known to promote brain function and boost energy so will not only give you vitality, but increased focus as well.

get more energy

nourishment

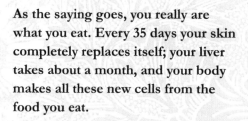

"The doctors of the future will no longer treat the human frame with drugs, but rather will cure and prevent disease with nutrition."

- Thomas Edison

As the saying goes, you really are what you eat. **Every 35 days your skin completely replaces itself; your liver takes about a month, and your body makes all these new cells from the food you eat.**

So what you eat literally becomes YOU. Therefore you are in the perfect position to decide what your body is made of by what you eat.

Nutrition is the key to overall health and proper nutrition is essential for us to look, feel and perform at our best. Nutrition is the fuel that we give to our bodies so we must eat quality food to gain energy, burn fat and maximise our performance on a daily basis.

Over the years I've collected all sorts of facts and tips about nutrition, from the best foods to fuel your body, ways to boost your metabolism and fine tune your digestion, to the foods that are insidiously sabotaging your wellbeing and ability to manage your weight. Here are some of the best to inspire you, to ditch any bad habits and invest in your health and wellbeing through making better choices.

WATER, WATER EVERYWHERE

WATER IS THE MIRACLE LIQUID, VITAL FOR GOOD HEALTH.
It helps you lose weight, keeps your muscles hydrated and can help suppress your appetite. Drink at least two litres of pure water every day and more during exercise and excessive sweating.

Ironically, the more water you drink the less likely you are to suffer fluid retention, bloating and puffiness. It flushes out accumulated toxins and excess water weight.

The fat-burning process of metabolism also needs water to work effectively. A clinical research centre in Berlin found that our fat-burning metabolism increases by 30 per cent within 10 minutes of drinking 500ml of water! So keep drinking!

Being well-hydrated also helps keep your skin clear, glowing and youthful - the simplest, cheapest beauty tip of all.

REV UP YOUR METABOLISM

We often think of our metabolism in terms of the potential for losing or gaining weight. Certainly, if someone metabolises food too quickly, they can't store energy in fat and muscle so will usually be thin. The reverse applies for people with a slow metabolism. But it's so much more than that.

METABOLISM IS LITERALLY THE POWERHOUSE OF THE BODY, breaking down what we eat and drink and rebuilding it into useful substances to provide energy to keep us going in every respect. So what we eat, how we eat it and what energy we expend has a huge impact on the process.

HERE ARE SOME TIPS:

EAT MORE OFTEN

Eat three larger, but not large, meals and about three healthy snacks a day to help fire up your fat-burning capacity. It also helps keep your appetite under control so you don't overeat or develop food cravings.

EAT LOTS OF VITAMIN-RICH PROTEIN

Eat lean beef, turkey, fish, chicken, tofu, nuts, beans, eggs, and low-fat dairy products and high-fibre foods. They increase your metabolism because your body burns the most calories digesting foods higher in these factors. Make protein at least 30% of your diet to get the metabolism-boosting effects.

EAT HIGH-FIBRE CARBS

Eat whole grain, high-fibre versions of foods such as bread, cereal and rice. Forget the virtually fibreless, highly-refined white stuff. High-fibre carbs burn more calories during digestion, help you feel full longer and trigger less fat-storing insulin than refined ones.

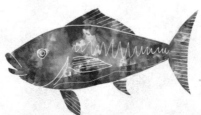

CONSUME LESS CAFFEINE

In the short term, a cup of coffee or tea (even green tea) can give your metabolism a spike, but too many caffeinated drinks can make you dehydrated and even mild dehydration can slow your metabolism. (I try to stick to one cup of coffee per day, in the morning and make sure I drink an extra litre of water to compensate).

ADD SPICE TO YOUR DIET

Spicy foods contain chemical compounds that can kick the metabolism into a higher gear temporarily boosting your metabolic rate. Eaten on a regular basis they may have a cumulative metabolic affect. Spices to add to your diet – say, to pasta, rice dishes or casseroles – include fresh or dried chilli, allspice, cardamom, cayenne pepper, cloves, coriander, curry powder, five-spice powder, galangal, garam masala, ginger, paprika, peppercorns (white, green or black) and turmeric.

STOP DIETING

Say no to crash diets (eating fewer than 1000 calories a day). I cannot stress enough how disastrous these are for your physical and emotional health and also your weight loss goals. You may drop weight in the short term, but it is mostly from muscle not fat. The less muscle mass you have, the slower your metabolism is, so your weight loss will quickly plateau. When you start eating more, you're more likely to gain the weight back quickly – and even more than before.

MOVE MORE

The more you move during the day, the more calories you burn. And working out in the morning has the added benefit of revving up your metabolism for the rest of your day. Start a cardio routine (walking, running, cycling or power yoga, for instance) and build some strength training into your schedule.

SWEET
POISON

One of the most disturbing areas of nutritional research would have to be the growing body of scientific evidence on the harmful effects of sugar. The truth is there is no physical need for added sugar in our diets. It is addictive, leads to cravings and over-eating, promotes poor dental health, increases your body fat, as well as increasing your risk of Type 2 diabetes, heart disease and all manner of other health problems.

We are born with a sweet tooth because we needed the bursts of energy it provided us to survive, but evolution did not prepare us for the abundance and ready availability of sugar that we have today.

My advice is to avoid drinks and snacks that contain added sugar or refined sweeteners, cut down the use of all sweeteners in your diet and have sugar-laden desserts occasionally rather than after every meal.

If I crave something sweet after a meal I usually go for a piece of high quality, plain dark chocolate with at least 70% cacao or my homemade chocolate bark.

The amount of sugar in it is small and if I let it slowly melt in my mouth I find that is all I need to curb my craving.

If you can't live without sweetness in your foods, there are some good alternatives to sugar - but, like sugar, they should be eaten only occasionally, not consumed all the time:

+ Raw honey, especially wild honey.
+ Organic maple syrup.
+ Dates.
+ Stevia.
  (A non-calorific sweetener made from an extract of the South American Stevia rebaudiana plant. It's extremely sweet, so easy does it).
+ Coconut sugar.
+ Molasses.

MAKE THE SWAP

So if your aim is to reduce your sugar intake, lose weight, have more energy or just be healthier, here are some of the swaps I recommend:

SWAP — YOUR DAILY COFFEE FOR A GLASS OF COCONUT WATER WITH A TEASPOON OF SPIRULINA FOR ADDED ENERGY WITHOUT THE CAFFEINE.

SWAP — SUGAR- LADEN FAT-FREE YOGHURT FOR FULL-FAT, OR LOW-FAT NATURAL YOGHURT.

SWAP — MANGOES, BANANAS AND PINEAPPLES FOR FRUIT WITH LOWER SUGAR CONTENT SUCH AS APPLES AND RED BERRIES.

SWAP — CALORIE-LADEN BANANA BREAD FOR FRUIT TOAST.

SWAP — THAT 3PM OVERLY-PROCESSED, HIGH-SALT PACKET OF CHIPS FOR SOME WHOLE WHEAT CRACKERS OR VEGETABLE STICKS WITH HUMMUS.

MAKE A GOOD START

Every day offers you the chance to do and be great, so start as you mean to finish and always, always, always eat a good breakfast to kick-start your metabolism and give you that much-needed energy to start your day. Breakfast is the most important meal of the day and it's worth getting up 15 minutes earlier to make something nourishing and delicious to savour at home or take to work.

Aim to have a good mix of carbohydrates, protein and good fats. And your choice of coffee, tea or spirulina coconut water!

there is
no love
More Sincere
than the
Love
of food

– GEORGE BERNARD SHAW –

coconut oats
parfait

Makes 1 serve
Prep time: 1-12 hrs

1/3 cup rolled oats
1 tbsp chia seeds
2 tbsp shredded
or flaked coconut
1 tsp vanilla extract

1 tbsp soaked and
chopped almonds
½ cup water
berries (to layer)

Add all ingredients together, except for
berries, in a glass jar. Let it sit overnight,
or for at least an hour. Layer the coconut
oats in a glass with the berries.

quinoa
porridge

Makes 4 serves
Prep time: 15 mins
Cook time: 20 mins

1 cup quinoa, soaked
1 cup water
1 cup coconut milk
½ tsp sea salt
2 tbsp coconut oil

1 tsp ground cinnamon
1 tbsp honey
2 tbsp dried
blueberries
2 tbsp pecans

Add quinoa, coconut milk and water to a pot
on high heat. When boiled, turn down to a
simmer, with the lid on.

After 15 mins check to see if all the liquid
has absorbed. Once it has, turn off the
heat, drape a tea towel over the top of the
pot, place the lid back on and let it sit for
another 10 mins.

Then mix through the rest of the ingredients.
Serve with grilled stonefruit, berries or
coconut milk.

pancakes

Prep time: 33 mins
Cook time: 15 mins

1 banana, mashed
2 eggs
1 tbsp chia seeds

2 tsp cinnamon
1 tsp vanilla extract
coconut oil (to cook)

In a bowl mash the banana, then add the eggs and whisk, incorporating the ingredients thoroughly. (To get a smoother mix, blend in a food processor).

Add in the rest of the ingredients, and allow to sit for at least half an hour.

In a hot pan on medium high heat, add 1 tsp of coconut oil.

Spoon the mix into the pan forming pancakes approx. 2 inches in diameter. Turn the heat down if oil is smoking.

After about 1 min, when the top of the pancake bubbles, flip the pancake over and cook for around another 30 seconds.

Drain on paper towel.

Clean the pan and add another teaspoon of coconut oil (if needed) before starting the next round of pancakes.

Serve drizzled with honey or maple syrup, and berries.

egg & veggie scramble

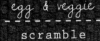

Makes 1 serve
Prep time: 15 mins
Cook time: 15 mins

2 eggs
½ bunch broccolini
1 carrot
1 cup grilled chicken
½ capsicum

2 tsp coconut oil
1 cup spinach
(you can use leftover veggies from dinner the night before)

Steam the carrot and broccolini until they are tender (approx. 8-10 mins).

Shred the cooked chicken.

Crack two eggs into a bowl, then whisk.

Add the capsicum, tomatoes, steamed vegetables and chicken to the egg mix.

Put a pan on medium-high heat with the coconut oil. When hot, add the egg mixture.

Stir the mixture in the pan until the eggs have become opaque. Serve on top of a bed of spinach or fresh sourdough.

lamb & mung bean loaf with
pepper & pomegranate sugo

vietnamese
rice paper rolls

Makes 2-4 serves
Prep time: 15 mins
Cook time: 30-40 mins

500g lamb mince
500g sweet potato, steamed & mashed
2 eggs
200g mung bean sprouts
1 carrot, grated
1 capsicum, diced
1 brown onion, diced
3 inch knob of ginger, minced
4 cloves garlic, minced

1 ½ tsp sea salt
1 tsp cracked black pepper
1 tsp paprika
1 ½ tsp cumin
1 tsp garam masala
½ tsp cinnamon
1 tsp turmeric
1 tbsp tamari
1 tbsp apple cider vinegar

In a bowl, incorporate all ingredients thoroughly. Press into a lined loaf tin and cook in a 170°C oven for around 30 mins, or until it has browned on top and the meat has released juices. Serve with pepper and pomegranate sugo.

pepper & pomegranate sugo

400g tomatoes (tinned or diced fresh)
1 brown onion, diced
4 cloves garlic, minced
1 tbsp coconut oil
1 tsp honey
½ tsp sea salt

2 tbsp pomegranate molasses
1 tsp cracked black pepper
½ tbsp tamari or salt-reduced soy sauce

Sauté onion with coconut oil in hot pan until softened. Add garlic and tomatoes, and stir, still on high heat, until fragrant. Add rest of ingredients, reduce to low heat, and allow to simmer for 10 mins.

capsicum soup

Makes 4 serves
Prep time: 15 mins
Cook time: 45 mins

4 tomatoes, halved
6 red capsicums, roughly chopped
2 red onions, peeled then roughly chopped
1 ½ tbsp fennel seeds
½ cup vegetable stock

1 bulb garlic, halved with skin on
1 tsp sea salt
1 tsp cracked black pepper
2 tbsp coconut oil

In a baking tray, mix together tomatoes, capsicum, onions, garlic and fennel seeds. Drizzle with coconut oil and season with salt and pepper. Roast in oven for 45 mins at 190°C, stirring well after 20 mins. Allow to cool for 15 mins. Squeeze out garlic cloves and remove peel. Blend in a high powered blender with ½ cup vegetable stock. Serve soup with poached chicken and spinach.

Makes 2 serves
Prep time: 30mins

6 sheets rice paper rounds
1 carrot, julienned
1 capsicum, deseeded, julienned
1 beetroot, peeled, julienned
100g bean or alfalfa sprouts
½ cup snow peas, julienned
1 chicken breast, cooked and cut into six strips
6 sprigs coriander, roots removed

Fill a large pot or saucepan with warm water. Dampen a clean tea towel with warm water and place over flat work surface.

Place one rice paper into the warm water for thirty seconds. Carefully remove and place onto the damp tea towel. Assemble approx. 1/6th of all the ingredients along the bottom centre of the rice paper, careful not to overfill. Fold ends in and roll up firmly to enclose filling. Repeat with remaining rice paper rounds and filling. Serve with a sweet chilli sauce or balsamic vinaigrette.

rainbow salad

Makes 2 serves
Prep time: 30 mins

1 carrot, julienned
1 capsicum, deseeded & julienned
4 radishes, thinly sliced
½ cup snow peas, julienned
1 cup salad rocket
2 cups baby spinach
1 cup sunflower sprouts
¼ cup dried blueberries

lime & chilli dressing

2 tbsp lime juice
½-1 large red chilli, deseeded and finely chopped
1 tsp raw honey
3 tbsp extra virgin olive oil

After prepping, combine all salad ingredients into a bowl. To make the dressing, combine all the dressing ingredients and allow to infuse for 5 mins before using. Toss through salad just before serving.

LET'S DO **LUNCH**

thai-style

----

coconut soup

Makes 2 serves Prep time: 15 mins Cook time: 25 mins

1 brown onion, finely sliced
2 tsp coconut oil
3 kaffir lime leaves, finely sliced
1 stalk lemongrass, finely sliced
1 inch piece fresh ginger, grated
½ inch piece turmeric, grated
¼ -1 red chilli,
depending on heat and taste preference

1 lime, zest and juice
1 can coconut milk
2 cups water
1 tbsp fish sauce
200g snow peas, julienned
200g shiitake mushrooms, sliced
½ bunch coriander, chopped

Add coconut oil to a pot on medium heat, and sauté onion until soft.
Then, add kaffir lime leaves, lemongrass, ginger, turmeric, chilli, lime zest and juice.
Cook for a further 5 mins, stirring regularly.
Add coconut milk and water. Simmer gently with the lid on for 15 mins, stirring regularly.
Add the fish sauce, snow peas and shiitake mushrooms and stir.
Simmer for a further 2 mins, add half of coriander, and then remove from heat.
Serve with seafood and garnish with rest of coriander.

grilled salmon with
----
celeriac mash & watercress salad

Makes 2 serves
Prep time: 10 mins
Cook time: 15-20 mins

grilled salmon

2 salmon fillets
2 tsp coconut oil
salt & pepper

In a plastic bag place all ingredients and shake to coat the salmon. On a medium-high grill plate, place salmon, skin-side down (if applicable).

Let cook, undisturbed until the fillet starts to release its juices, approx. 10 mins. Turn over and cook for a further 5 mins, or to your preference.

Serve with lemon wedges, cracked black pepper, celeriac mash and watercress salad.

celeriac mash

1 large celeriac, peeled & roughly chopped

3 garlic cloves
salt & pepper, to taste
1 tbsp goat chevre

Steam celeriac and garlic over pot of boiling water until celeriac is tender.

Add salt, pepper, and goats chevre, then mash until well combined.

watercress salad

1 bunch of watercress, roots removed and washed thoroughly
2 tbsp capers

2 lemons
2 tbsp extra virgin olive oil
1 tsp cracked black pepper
sea salt, to taste

Remove peel from one of the lemons, and cut into segments, removing all seeds. In a bowl combine watercress, lemon segments, approx 1 tsp of lemon zest, and capers. To make the dressing, mix together the juice from the remaining lemon, olive oil and salt. Serve with dressing and cracked black pepper.

crab cakes with
asian coleslaw

Makes 2 serves

Prep time: 15 mins

Cook time: 20 mins

300g cooked sand crab meat
200g chicken breast,
cooked and shredded
1 small brown onion,
finely diced
1 kaffir lime leaf
1/3-1 red chilli
(depending on taste)

½ tsp ginger, grated
½ tsp turmeric, grated
1 lime, juice and zest
2 inch piece of lemongrass,
finely sliced
1 tbsp coconut oil
¼ cup coconut milk
¼ cup chopped coriander

½ tsp sea salt
1 tsp black pepper
1 tbsp tamari
or salt-reduced soy sauce
1 egg
extra coconut oil for cooking

In a medium hot pan sauté together onion, kaffir lime leaf, ginger, turmeric, lime, lemongrass with coconut oil. Once softened and fragrant, blend in a food processor until smooth.

Add the rest of the ingredients to the onion paste. Mix thoroughly, mixture should form a ball when pressed in your hands. Heat coconut oil in pan on medium heat. Roll mixture into balls and press onto hot pan. Cook on each side until browned, about 2 mins, then drain on paper towel. Serve with Asian coleslaw.

asian coleslaw

½ purple cabbage, finely sliced
¼ sugarloaf cabbage,
finely sliced
1 carrot, julienned
½ capsicum, julienned
4 sprigs mint, leaves chopped

¼ bunch coriander,
finely chopped
2 tbsp extra virgin olive oil
1 lime, juice
salt and pepper to taste

Mix olive oil, lime juice, salt and pepper together. In a large bowl mix all salad ingredients. Toss through dressing when ready to serve.

tamari chicken kebabs with
grilled veggie stacks

Makes 2 serves
Prep time: 12 hrs
Cook time: 15 mins

chicken kebabs

2 chicken breasts, diced into 2 cm cubes
2 tbsp tamari
1 tbsp extra virgin olive oil
1 lemon, juice
2 cloves garlic, minced
1 tsp ground coriander
1 tsp ground cumin
1 tsp fresh ginger, grated

Combine all marinade ingredients.

Place chicken cubes into a bowl, and stir through marinade.

Allow to marinate overnight.

Thread chicken onto kebab skewers.

Grill on a medium hot grill plate for approx. 5 mins each side, or until chicken is cooked through. Serve with grilled vegetable stacks.

Alternatively, thread button mushrooms and capsicums onto skewers along with chicken.

grilled veggie stacks

1 large eggplant,
sliced into 1 inch circles
1 zucchini,
sliced into 1 inch circles
6 squash, sliced into
half widthwise
½ orange sweet potato,
sliced into 1 inch circles
1 large red capsicum,
sliced into 6 strips
6 button mushrooms
100g salad rocket
coconut oil to grill
salt & pepper
fresh basil

In a grill pan on low heat, pour a little coconut oil and cook the sweet potato for 10 mins each side, until tender. Season and turn the heat to high, charring it quickly on each side.

Sprinkle salt and pepper over all the vegetables, and cook in the same grill pan on medium high heat until they have tenderised and charred on each side. Oil the pan when needed.

Stack the veggies and rocket, beginning with the largest and finishing with the smallest.

Top with fresh basil, and use a toothpick to secure if necessary.

DELISH

lychee

----

cheesecake

Makes 4 serves   Prep time: 3 ½ hrs   Cook time: 10 mins

cheesecake crumb
1 cup rolled oats
½ cup dessicated coconut
1 tsp vanilla extract
2 tbsp coconut oil

lychee labne
½ cup lychee juice
2 tsp vanilla extract
1 ½ cups natural,
unsweetened yoghurt

lychee jelly
600g lychees, peeled & deseeded
2 tbsp natural, unsweetened yoghurt
10g gelatine powder or 5 (2g) gelatine
sheets (preferably Bernard Jensen
or Great Lakes Brand)
100 mL boiling water

At least 1 hour before, peel and deseed lychees, and hang flesh in a mesh strainer over a bowl. Keep the juice.

TO MAKE THE CRUMB, heat oven to 150°C. Toast oats in oven for 10 mins.

Stir coconut through the oats, and return to oven for another 5 mins, or until the coconut has browned slightly and become fragrant.

Set aside to cool before stirring through vanilla extract.

TO MAKE THE LABNE, measure the lychee juice extracted from the hanging lychees.

If you don't have at least ½ cup, gently squeeze the lychee flesh until you do.

In a bowl, mix lychee juice, yoghurt, and vanilla extract.

Place in fridge until needed.

TO MAKE THE JELLY, boil 100mL water.

If using gelatine powder - pour boiling water into a wide dish, and spread required amount of gelatine powder over surface. Allow to dissolve in the water, stirring occasionally.

If using gelatine sheets – bloom gelatine sheets covered in ice water for 5 mins.

Once water has boiled, lift out gelatine sheets from ice water, squeeze out excess water and place into cup with boiling water.

Stir to dissolve.

Place lychee flesh into a food processor, along with yoghurt. Blend until smooth.

Pour into a bowl, and add the dissolved gelatine and water mix. Stir well to distribute the gelatine through the mix.

ASSEMBLE the cheesecake as efficiently as you can before the jelly sets.

In four wide glasses, cover the bottom with cheesecake crumb then pour the liquid lychee jelly over the top, filling two inches from the top of the glass.

Put cheesecakes into the fridge and allow to set for at least 2 hrs.

Before serving, fill the rest of the cheesecake glass with lychee labne and top with fresh lychees and mint.

chocolate pistachio
strawberries

Makes 2-4 serves   Prep time: 50 mins

70% dark chocolate   1-2 punnets of
200g pistachios, shelled fresh strawberries
& finely chopped

You will need three bowls, (one for the chocolate, one for berries and one for nuts).

Melt chocolate in a large skillet with water and heat to just below simmering.

Place the chocolate in a heat-proof bowl, such as stainless steel and place the bowl in the water. Gently and continually stir the chocolate, while keeping the water below simmering.

Line a tray with baking paper.

Dip strawberries into chocolate then dip into pistachios and place on baking tray.

Pop tray in the fridge for 40 mins to cool.

berry
ice-cream

Makes 2 serves
Prep time: 5 mins

150g frozen blueberries or other berries
3 tbsp natural, unsweetened yoghurt
1 tsp vanilla extract

Blend all ingredients into a food processor, or until smooth. Top with bee pollen, your favourite nut mix or melted dark chocolate. Best eaten immediately.

banana
ice-cream

Makes 3 serves
Prep time: 5 mins

3 bananas, frozen
3 tbsp natural, unsweetened yoghurt
1 tsp freshly ground cinnamon

Carefully chop frozen bananas into small chunks. Blend all ingredients into a food processor until smooth. Serve immediately, or place in sealed contained in freezer and preferably use within two days. Top with bee pollen, your favourite nut mix or melted dark chocolate.

coconut & maple
black rice pudding

Makes 4 serves Prep time: 5 mins Cook time: 1 hr

1 cup black rice   1 tsp freshly ground
2 ½ cups coconut milk   cinnamon
1 tsp vanilla extract   1-3 tbsp maple syrup
¼ cup dessicated   (depending on taste)
coconut

coconut caramel

2 cups coconut milk   1 tbsp maple syrup

To make the coconut caramel, place 2 cups of coconut milk and maple syrup into a heavy-based pot. Cook for around 1 hr on the lowest heat setting available. Stir approximately every 5 mins.

While the coconut milk is caramelising, cook the rice pudding. Rinse the black rice thoroughly, and then place it into a pot along with 2 ½ cups of coconut milk. Cover with a lid, bring to the boil, and then reduce to a simmer. Stir frequently.

After 30 mins add the rest of the ingredients to the pudding and continue to simmer for another 10mins.

Add 2 tbsp of water if all the liquid has absorbed but rice is still not cooked.

Serve warm or cold, topped with the coconut caramel and grilled nectarines, blueberries or toasted coconut.

chocolate
mousse

Makes 4 serves   Prep time: 2 ½ hrs

1 ½ cups coconut   3 egg whites, room
cream (approx. 2 cans   temperature
coconut cream in   ½-1 cup honey
fridge the night before) (depending on taste)
¼ cup cacao powder

Place the egg whites into a bowl of an electric mixer (alternatively can use hand held). Using the whisk attachment, whisk whites until they form firm peaks (when turn whisk upside down, peaks will hold, but tips may fold back). Scoop out into another bowl, and refrigerate until required.

Open the refrigerated cans of coconut cream and skim off the thick, white coconut cream, leaving the liquid at the bottom (this liquid can be used in another recipe that calls for coconut milk). Put this coconut cream into a clean mixer bowl, and, again, using the whisk attachment, whisk for around 5 mins, adding the honey gradually. The coconut cream should increase in volume.

Sift the cacao powder into the whipped coconut cream, and fold in well. Then, gently fold in stiff egg whites, one third at a time. Allow the mousse to set in individual ramekins or a piping bag for at least 2 hrs before serving.

Serve alongside fresh fruit.

THE *Sweet* SPOT

coconut water

peach

mixed nuts

Power
SNACKS

2 eggs

hummus

½ carrot, 2 sticks of celery, ½ dozen green beans

hummus (makes 6 serves)

400g chickpeas, canned
or soaked and boiled
2 garlic cloves, peeled
2 tbsp tahini

1 tbsp extra virgin olive oil
1 tsp sea salt
½ tsp pepper
1 lemon, juice

Put all ingredients into a food
processor, and blend until smooth.

Taste to see if needs more seasoning
or lemon juice.

peanut butter & strawberries

smashed avocado (lemon, salt & pepper), radish & alfafa sprouts

tahini, spinach & tomato

chevre, figs & honey

My thoughts on BEAUTY

— MY ROUTINE —

*My philosophy on beauty boils down to this:
keep it simple, organic and as close to nature as possible.*

Cosmetic companies the world over will tell you to use this cream, that serum and maybe even offer to laser this and put a needle in that.

But I believe without a doubt, that the biggest and best beauty secrets are to nourish your body with good food, move your body every day, have the confidence to believe in yourself; and get plenty of water and sleep. Oh, and be happy and stay out of the sun!

There is not a doubt in my mind that how you treat your body on the inside is truly reflected in how you look on the outside. All the products in the world cannot replace the radiance of skin that has been nourished from within.

I don't really have any beauty secrets, but I do stick to the same routine because when it comes to skin, I believe consistency is important.

One of the most important things as far as your skin is concerned, is to make sure you stay hydrated. Your skin dehydrates during the night so I always have a glass of water by the side of my bed to drink as soon as I wake up.

Because I exercise first thing in the morning I will just splash my face with water, dab on a little eye cream to hydrate around my eyes, moisturise (put on a little sunscreen if I am exercising outside) and I'm off.

Exercise plays a vital role in healthy skin. It not only lifts your mood but it aids your detoxification processes by stimulating lymphatic drainage and eliminating any nasty toxins through sweating.

I find beginning my day with some stretches followed by a workout like walking, running, cycling or swimming is a great way to get my circulation moving and kick-start my day (and metabolism!).

"to be beautiful is to be yourself"

If you are feeling stressed, I recommend passive exercise. Yoga is great because, as well as being a powerful workout, it also makes you relax while at the same time helping to detox, build muscle and flexibility. One of the things I love most about yoga is the focus on breathing. Did you know by simply getting more oxygen into your blood through deep breathing your skin takes on a natural vibrancy for hours afterwards?

I also recommend exfoliating as part of your daily ritual. I dry body brush every morning – and sometimes evening – to boost my lymphatic system before showering. I use a gentle exfoliant on my face every day and a sugar scrub on my body two to three times a week. I find exfoliation is essential for radiant beauty because it speeds up cell renewal to give you a fresher, smoother, more youthful-looking skin.

I must admit I only wear makeup when it's absolutely necessary. I'm lucky that I don't have to wear it for work, so I like to keep my skin as clean and clear of products as possible. Most days I just put a tinted moisturiser with sunscreen over my regular day moisturiser, brush on a little mascara and lip-gloss and I'm good to go.

When it comes to looking your best let's not forget the importance of sleep, and getting your eight hours on a regular basis is essential for repairing your skin and giving your body the time it needs to restore and detoxify.

Most of us spend a third of our time in bed, so consider purchasing a silk pillowcase. They not only add that little bit of luxury every woman deserves but they also prevent sleep creases, skin stretching and hair damage through the night.

Long the secret of film divas, silk allows the skin to 'glide' along the pillow so your face rests comfortably without forming creases which effectively 'iron in' wrinkles.

Silk pillowcases also cause less friction when you move around at night meaning less hair tangling and pulling. This in turn means less hair loss and better-looking hair in the morning. Silk keeps straight hair straighter and blow-dries last longer.

Finally, doing what you love; having confidence, feeling good about yourself and being happy gives you a glow and radiance you could never buy at any beauty counter.

As legendary screen beauty Sophia Loren once said:

"Nothing makes a woman more beautiful than the belief she is beautiful."

And I'm not going to argue with that!

YOUR SKIN IS THE WINDOW to your inner health and when your body is in poor shape, your complexion – and how beautiful you look on the outside – can be the first place it shows.

FOR A YOUTHFUL GLOW, sparkling smile, shiny hair and general feeling of wellbeing, good nutrition and finding time to exercise and care for your body is key.

The good news is that it's never too late to get started; so if your track record to-date hasn't been so good, RESTORING YOUR RADIANCE can be as simple as making a few changes to your lifestyle, diet and skincare routine.

START THE DAY WITH THE GLASS OF WARM WATER AND LEMON JUICE (half a squeezed lemon with approximately three times as much warm water) to hydrate and oxygenate your body so it feels energised and refreshed.

This is the perfect start for the day as you not only will be balancing your ph, and boosting your immune system, but purifying your blood at the same time.

Forget expensive face creams and remind yourself that PURE WATER IS AN EXCELLENT ANTI-AGEING TONIC that will keep your skin hydrated, supple and fresh. Also when your body is properly hydrated it makes any fine lines and wrinkles less pronounced — and who doesn't want that!

GOOD NUTRITION equals healthy, youthful skin, so a good place to start is by reducing the amount of sugar, white flour and processed foods you have in your diet, and begin eating A BALANCED WHOLE FOOD DIET containing low GI carbohydrates, high quality proteins and loads of non-starchy vegetables — to help boost your energy levels, improve your skin and minimise sugar cravings.

I KNOW YOU HAVE HEARD IT A MILLION TIMES, BUT LET ME REMIND YOU THAT WATER IS VITAL FOR BEAUTY.

FRESH FOODS LOADED WITH vitamins, minerals and antioxidants will give your skin far more ammunition against lines, wrinkles, dryness and crepiness than expensive creams and beauty treatments.

AVOCADOS ARE AMAZING, as they contain 20 vitamins (especially E) and minerals that your skin needs to glow.

TOMATOES, POMEGRANATES, LEAFY GREEN VEGETABLES, BROCCOLI, BERRIES, GRAPES AND CITRUS FRUITS are also excellent sources, along with whole grains and nuts.

Other great foods that have been shown to STRENGTHEN THE SKIN include turkey, salmon and other fish high in OMEGA-3 FATTY ACIDS, soybeans and soy products (eg. tofu).

It's also a good idea to preserve and KEEP YOUR DIGESTIVE SYSTEM HEALTHY WITH A DAILY PROBIOTIC. This can be taken as a supplement (I recommend liquid form) or by including yoghurt, tempeh (a soybean patty) or miso in your diet.

IF YOUR DIGESTION IS SLUGGISH, toxins in the form of undigested food can accumulate and pollute your body. That not only effects your overall vitality, but can also leave you feeling tired and sluggish and your skin and hair looking dull.

PROBIOTICS HELP RESTORE OUR INTERNAL BALANCE by improving digestive and liver functions, improving resistance to allergies and vitamin synthesis, and improving the absorption of nutrients whilst eliminating bloating and heartburn.

GOOD DIGESTION IS VITAL FOR LOOKING GOOD. A DIGESTIVE TRACT IN TOP WORKING ORDER WILL EFFECTIVELY TRANSFORM FOOD INTO ENERGY AND ELIMINATE TOXINS FROM YOUR BODY.

A FEW OF MY
FAVOURITE THINGS

As I said, I'm a low maintenance kind of girl when it
comes to beauty, but there are some products I use every
day that I just can't live without.

Because I like to be outdoors, top of my list would have to be
sunscreen. I wear 30+ sunscreen every day, no exceptions. And I always
have an extra tube in my bag just in case I need to top it up during the
day. It is one of the most important anti-ageing tools you can use, not
to mention it helps reduce the risk of developing skin cancer. Choose
sunscreen formulas that contain a high level of SPF that are broad spectrum
– with UVA and UVB protection.

While fresh air and vitamin D from sunshine are essential for good health
they are not that great for your skin. Exposure to UV rays accelerates
the ageing process leading to rough, dry skin, lines and wrinkles and,
often, uneven pigmentation.

To reduce any pigmentation that you already have, and
prevent new spots forming, I recommend a vitamin
C serum used after cleansing and prior to
applying your moisturiser.

FACE

After my morning workout, I shower and cleanse my face and décolletage with a light exfoliating cleanser. I make sure it's mild enough to use every day because I find daily exfoliating gives my skin a radiance that regular cleansing never has.

I'm totally addicted to natural products so follow cleansing with an anti-ageing serum with ingredients such as vitamin C, an organic eye cream and a great moisturiser. Over that I apply another tinted moisturiser if I'm not wearing make-up - which is most days. I love tinted moisturiser because it evens out my skin tone and gives my skin even more nourishment and SPF30+.

Rosewater spray is another product that I use all the time, it's wonderful for topping up my skin's hydration through the day and I keep a bottle in my handbag for when I am in air conditioning for extended periods of time or travelling.

When I'm at home I keep it in the fridge because I find putting it chilled on my skin is both refreshing and soothing.

I use rose hip oil as a night moisturiser for my face, neck, décolletage and under my eyes. This nourishing oil contains powerful antioxidants and essential vitamins to replenish my skin's elasticity and softness. When my skin is dry I also cleanse with rose hip oil to hold in moisture. This is great during the summer months because you can wash away any impurities while keeping your skin's natural moisture balance intact.

I also swear by vitamin E oil on my lips at night to give them a big hydration boost while I sleep. And I always have a tube of vitamin E cream by the side of my bed to put on my hands at night before I go to sleep

For a natural blemish booster I dab a few drops of tea tree oil or organic coconut oil on my skin. Tea tree oil is famous for its drying properties and coconuts have anti-fungal and anti-bacterial properties that will banish those blemishes pronto!

BODY

Okay, so I've already mentioned that I dry body brush every day and exfoliate on a regular basis, but it is equally important to make sure you moisturise every inch of your body as well.

I loooove coconut oil as a moisturiser; it not only smells delicious, but it acts as a nourishing, anti-ageing, moisturising multi-vitamin for my skin.

If my skin feels especially dehydrated, or I want something a little less fragrant, I use Bio-Oil - a beautifully light, easily absorbed dry oil containing plant extracts and vitamins. I find it really helpful for keeping lines and dryness at bay, and it makes my skin feel extremely soft and supple.

I also put papaya cream on my hands and lips regularly throughout the day. As well as being a rich (and cheap) moisturiser, papaya contains a natural exfoliating enzyme, which makes my skin and lips feel super smooth.

PAMPERING

What girl doesn't love to be pampered? I do try to indulge myself with a salon treatment when I can spare the time - which I hate to admit is usually when I am on holidays! And then I pretty much just want to try everything!

I have a regular massage - usually once a month - but do most of my masks and facials at home.

That way I can be sure that all of the ingredients and nutrients applied to my skin are as close to their natural state as possible and I can just relax and enjoy them in the comfort of my own surroundings.

HAIR

I have been massaging coconut oil into my scalp and through my hair prior to washing for a while now and I couldn't be happier with how much softer my hair looks and feels - not to mention how good it smells! Now I am committed to a routine of treating my hair with coconut oil at least once a week.

I also love organic argan oil, and put it through my hair to give it some extra shine after styling. I also find just putting a little in the ends of my hair before I go to bed makes my hair look and feel better in the morning.

WHEN IT COMES TO BEAUTY TREATMENTS I LIKE NOTHING BETTER THAN TAKING NATURAL INGREDIENTS FROM MY KITCHEN AND APPLYING THEM TO MY FACE AND BODY ... THAT WAY I CAN BE SURE THAT THERE ARE NO NASTY CHEMICALS INVOLVED AND I GUESS IT JUST MAKES ME FEEL GOOD THAT I CAN TAKE THE GOODNESS OF NATURE AND USE IT TO NOURISH MY BODY ON THE OUTSIDE AS WELL.

There are just so many beauty benefits to be found in nature:

Avocados have been used for centuries and are the key ingredient in hair and skincare management due to their rich supply of vitamins and minerals. Full of vitamins B, C and E, avocados have the ability to slow down the aging process and moisturise your skin from the inside out.

Bananas and oatmeal can also do wonders for your skin – banana contains vitamins B6, B2 and B12 which help to reduce skin inflammation whilst making your skin soft and supple. Oatmeal is often used as a gentle exfoliant but can also be used to balance and calm a more sensitive skin.

Here are some of my favourite DIY beauty recipes for you to try and possibly include in your own beauty rituals.

BLACKHEADS BE GONE!

Banish those blackheads in 5 mins flat, with this quick and easy skin remedy. All you need is half a lemon and 3-4 drops of raw honey. Rub the lemon on your face, emphasising those problem areas (nose, chin, etc.). Leave the lemon and honey mixture on face for 5 mins, and rinse with cold water. You will see results immediately as the lemon juice fades any marks/ spots and the honey helps restore moisture back to that beautiful face of yours.

CROWN SUGAR COCONUT **BODY SCRUB**

1 TBSP RAW HONEY

1 CUP BROWN SUGAR

1/2 CUP SEA SALT

2 TBSP COCONUT OIL

2 TBSP FRESH LEMON JUICE

PLUS 1 TBSP OF YOUR FAVOURITE ESSENTIAL OIL

Combine ingredients in a bowl until it forms a paste. Apply to moist skin in a circular motion using your fingertips to help get rid of dead skin cells. Rinse off with warm water. Nourish your skin with your fav moisturiser for super smooth, glowing skin.

HONEY & OAT **FACIAL**

2 TBSP NATURAL YOGHURT

1 TBSP RAW HONEY

SQUEEZE OF LEMON JUICE

2 TBSP DRY OATMEAL

1 TBSP GROUND ALMONDS

Combine ingredients in a bowl to form the exfoliating facial scrub. Massage gently onto face and rinse with warm water. Finish with some moisturiser.

DIY BEAUTY RECIPES

BALANCING AVOCADO **FACE MASK**

3 TBSP GREEN CLAY POWDER

1 SMALL AVOCADO, MASHED

1 TSP FRESH LEMON JUICE

1/2 SMALL CUCUMBER, FINELY GRATED

Combine ingredients in a small bowl. Cover and chill for at least 30 mins. With clean, dry skin apply a thick layer to your face and neck, avoiding the eye and lip areas. Leave for 10-15 mins and wipe skin clean with a damp cloth.

EXFOLIATING **BREAKFAST MASK**

1 TBSP RAW HONEY

1 TBSP GREEK YOGHURT

1/4 BANANA, MASHED

Combine ingredients in a bowl, and apply to face for 15-20 mins. Rinse off with cool water and pat dry face. That's it. The yoghurt and banana work together to exfoliate the skin, while the honey has antibacterial and mosturising properties to give you that luminous glow.

BUILDING A BUSINESS
EVOLUTION OF LORNA JANE

You might have heard the media referring to me as a Fitness Guru or an Exercise Queen and sometimes even a Workout Icon, and though it sounds impressive and makes for a good headline at the time, I'm actually none of the above.

I'm just an ordinary girl who happens to have found what I love to do (my purpose in life), practised what I do every day, and have, over time become pretty good at it.

But what I want you to know is that I'm no different from you. I have my struggles, my frustrations and fears, along with my hopes, goals and dreams. I've had good days and some really bad ones. I've made some spectacularly good decisions and some pretty bad ones too. I'm very human, in fact I'm just a girl working hard to make the best of every day, trying to be a good wife, daughter, sister and friend while hoping in some way to make a difference in people's lives.

In the early days of Lorna Jane it was just me, and I did absolutely everything. But as my business grew I slowly started to introduce new people to complement the skills that I had and have managed over time to build a strong and inspiring team who share my vision and passion, not only for creating amazing active wear, but to inspire and promote Active Living as a vehicle to live a happy and fulfilling life.

I'm often asked what it's like to build a business and work alongside your husband and I guess most people think it would be hard and that it would lead to arguments and disharmony.

For Bill and I it is exactly the opposite. We work extremely well together and see it as a chance to love and support each other in every aspect of our life together. It also helps that our talents complement each other and he is no more likely to offer me design advice than I would care to manage a sales meeting or draw up the strategic plan for our US expansion.

We stick to what we are good at but value each other's opinion in all areas of our business.

it just started out as satisfying my own need for activewear.
it wasn't until i shared them with everyone else that i knew
i had a winning formula on my hands.

Looking back at where Lorna Jane started, where it came from and what it represents today, I realise just how far we have come, how much we have achieved and what an incredible business we have created.

When I started this business over 23 years ago, active-wear concept stores just didn't exist; now we have over 140 Lorna Jane stores worldwide. There were the big brands such as Nike, Adidas and Puma, but their focus was predominantly shoes and they were mainly to be found in big-box, male-dominated sports stores.

I didn't know of any other women's only active-wear labels that were available, and there certainly wasn't anyone doing anything remotely fashionable or feminine in the marketplace.

———————————————

The 1st Lorna Jane logo

▼

I began designing active-wear at a time when it wasn't even seen as a 'category'. Which is really quite amazing when you consider how huge the fitness industry was at the time with fitness centres opening on every street corner and aerobic classe attendance at an all time high.

My first 'store' in a fitness studio

And to think it all began on my dining room table, one weekend when I decided to pull apart my favourite-fitting swimsuit to make something to wear for my next class because I felt that anyone (even me with little to no sewing or design experience) could create something better than the current market had to offer. And you know what - I WAS RIGHT!

Just by making bespoke outfits for myself, and wearing them to teach my classes, I created a demand for this new innovation in workout wear that found me just a few months later quitting my day job and following my heart to build the Lorna Jane brand that you all know and love today.

Over the years, Lorna Jane has grown into a brand that inspires women all over the world to be fit and healthy. And through its actions, philosophies and reputation, it has created a whole new category that represents a modern and successful way to live your life.

This coveted and life-changing space is called:

ACTIVE LIVING

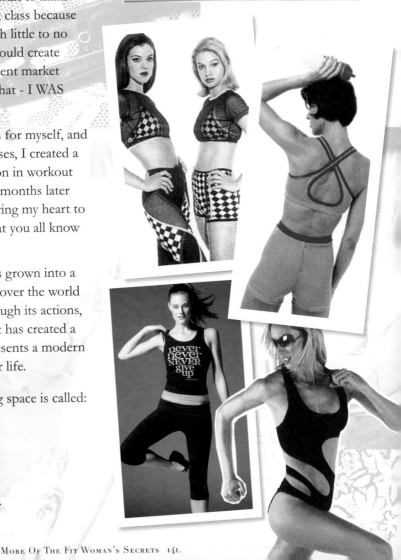

your dream is the best plan

I believe if you have a dream that you are truly passionate about, that ignites your senses, sets your heart racing and, of course is humanly possible, then you are more than halfway there when it comes to making it become a reality.

If this dream is 'YOUR REASON TO EXIST' as my business is to me, I believe you don't need a step-by-step plan to get started. You should just take your vision and use your incredible willpower to make it a reality.
If your dreams are anything like mine, I simply can't stopping thinking about them and am absolutely clear on what has to be done to achieve them — no business plan required!

Let's face it, you could spend hours, days, weeks, and even months over-analysing a situation, trying to put the pieces together and speculating what would, should and could happen. Or you could just get started!

Too often if you wait for 'the perfect time', 'the perfect building', or 'the perfect business plan' you may miss the opportunity and never begin. My philosophy in business is simple, just put one foot in front of the other, throw away any excuses and get started.

Your dream is the best plan

Don't restrict your thinking to what
other people are already doing in the
marketplace, use your imagination and
do things in your own unique way.
There may have been some who thought I
was crazy to believe I could actually
sell active wear from the floor of a
gym and even crazier to even imagine
that the same active-wear would go
on to be the leading women's active
wear brand in Australia. But it did,
because I refused to limit my thinking
and believed in the product enough to
know that if I could just get women
to see it, they would want to wear it
— whether it was in a shop or simply
displayed on the floor of a fitness
centre.

The most important thing, in my
opinion, is to have an innovative
idea and a product that creates
demand, then simply scrape the
essentials together and get started.
Put whatever money you've got (or
can borrow without over-extending
yourself) where your mouth is and
chase your dream.

But remember that it takes risk for
anything to actually happen, so don't
hold back, be daring, step out of
your comfort zone and do it with great
passion and gusto. My business, and
where I am today, is living proof that
anything truly is possible when you
are willing to give it 'your all'!

I also think that at the end
of our lives we will be more
disappointed by the things we
didn't do than by the things we
did — so we owe it to ourselves
to at least give it a go.

My Philosophies

If I could describe my business and life philosophy in one sentence, it would have to be:

"Do what you love and success will come."

I have always had a passion for fashion and fitness and the fact that I have been able to combine the two things I love and build a successful business doing it, has been a dream come true for me.

There are a number of other philosophies and practices that have guided me in both business and life, that have motivated me through good times and bad, and kept me on track.

SO HERE ARE A FEW THAT I HOPE WILL HELP YOU ON YOUR LIFE JOURNEY AS WELL:

There's a saying:

"The harder you work, the luckier you become."

And it's so true. Unless you're one in a million, you won't get lucky sitting around waiting for something amazing to happen. You simply have to go out on a limb, put in the work and create your own luck!

When it comes to your dreams

"Don't talk about it, do it!"

Making a dream come true takes a great deal of hard work, determination and planning so if you really want to see your dreams become your reality, stop talking about it and get going!

"Make 20 good decisions a day."

The girl who started Lorna Jane was much more cautious and I guess not overly confident when it came to making those 'can't turn back' decisions. I had no business home runs to boast about and every challenge was a new experience for me. With so many friends and family offering well-intended advice, it only fed my indecision. I had to develop strength to make decisions based on what felt right TO ME, to develop a trust in my instincts and rid myself of any doubts in order to move forward and achieve great things. And I have to say, the more 'Good Decisions' I made, the more confident I have became. Over the years I have made some great decisions as well as some poor choices and bold mistakes, all of which I have learned from greatly. Now I aim to make 20 good decisions every day (and no bad ones of course!)

"Don't be afraid to fail. Don't be afraid to try."

I have learnt that if you continue to do the same thing day in, day out you will obviously get the same result and remain the same. Don't be afraid to step out of your comfort zone and try new things even if you risk failure or embarrassment because it is only through trying and failing that you have a chance to try and succeed.

"The ones who are crazy enough to think they can change the world are the ones who do."

I love to be around people with Big Ideas, Bold Dreams and Huge Imaginations. It is only by spending time with these amazing visionaries that we learn to stretch our own minds and hope for the seemingly unachievable. And it's only when the initial response to your Big Idea is to tell you that it's impossible that you know you are really onto something!

"Learn something new every day."

Stretching your personal boundaries and improving the way you think means you will always be living an amazing life. This goes back to the practice of reading every day. One idea read in a book could transform the way you think about something, see the world or how you live. Too many people never pick up a book after they leave school and miss out on so much of the world. Don't be one of them.

OVERCOMING FEAR

My biggest fear in life and in business is not thinking BIG ENOUGH – not taking those chances and, as a result, living a small life.

I believe you can't improve what you do or how you live your life unless you are willing to take risks and do the things that scare you.

Too many people do the same thing day after day – eat the same breakfast, talk to the same people, watch the same TV shows.

THERE'S A SAYING THAT I LOVE:

"IF YOU KEEP ON DOING WHAT YOU'VE ALWAYS DONE, YOU'LL KEEP ON GETTING WHAT YOU'VE ALWAYS GOT."

I mean honestly, how can you expect change or improvement in your life if you are not prepared to make changes first? Of course things get tough and tricky at times, and it's inevitable you will feel some fear, but the way I get through is that I don't lose sight of why I started this journey in the first place.

Always remember why you set out to do what you're doing. If you get hooked on recognition, wanting to be viewed as being successful and better than other people or just needing attention, you will lose sight of your goals and you won't be as successful as you could be if you stayed focused.

BE FEARLESS.

When it comes to your dreams, stay true to who you are and what you want to do. Then believe me, there is nothing really to be afraid of.

DON'T FOLLOW YOUR DREAMS *chase* THEM

Be confident:

Too many days are wasted comparing ourselves, our success and where we are in life with others. Everybody has their own strengths and weaknesses and to be successful and overcome fear, we need to accept everything we are - and aren't - and move forward and create our own story.

feel the fear & DO it *anyway*

GETTING INSPIRED

>>>>>>>>>>>)(<<<<<<<<<<<<

I'm often asked how I stay inspired and motivated to keep growing and improving my business. And I honestly think that there are a lot of people who think I keep innovating and moving Lorna Jane forward to increase its value and create more wealth.

The truth is that I have a wonderful life and have achieved a level of success that I am proud of, but the reason I keep working, the reason I am so passionate about Lorna Jane and everything that it stands for is because I am actually

IN LOVE WITH IT!

I LOVE

designing innovative, fit and fashionable active wear

I LOVE

being the founder and face of a brand that inspires women to lead a fit and active life

I LOVE

promoting my Move Nourish Believe Philosophy

I LOVE

meeting customers and hearing their stories about the difference Lorna Jane has made in their lives

From the beginning, my greatest inspiration has always been my customers. Maybe it stems back to how I started my business in the gym, or because we opened our own stores and I would meet and chat with my customers on a daily basis. I am not entirely sure, but I do know that there is no better feeling for me than seeing a woman wearing Lorna Jane.

I love to see how she has put her outfit together, what shoes she is wearing with it and what accessories she has added to create her overall look.

I love to talk to my customers and give them insights into why we have designed certain features and the benefits they can find in particular products. I also like to get their feedback so that I can continue to give them the products they are looking for in their active lives.

I also like to talk about Active Living and the Move Nourish Believe philosophy. I have seen it change so many lives (mine included) and have this unstoppable, dare I say addiction to talking about and inspiring other women to experience it for themselves.

A manifesto is a public proclamation of what you intend to do with your future and intention is what brings purpose, meaning and significance to life.

By simply writing a manifesto you are making a promise to yourself and the rest of the world about who you are and what you are going to do with your life.

At Lorna Jane we have a manifesto that we put in our stores to let all of our customers know who we are and what we stand for. It outlines our values and is a constant reminder for us all to live by those values and keep the spirit of our culture alive.

I also have my own manifesto – or dream list – that reminds me every day what I value most in life and serves as a constant reminder for me to stay true and live authentically.

By writing your own manifesto you will remind yourself of everything you stand for and what you value in life. It should be a beautiful, inspiring, crazy, wonderful *"stretch document"* to remind you of all you want to achieve and experience for the rest of your life.

Make it public and use it as a constant reminder for you and the rest of the world proclaiming what you stand for, what you value and what you are going to do.

MY MANIFESTO

I believe in DREAMS.

I believe in WORKING HARD and reaching for the STARS.

I believe in LAUGHING, laughing ALOT.

I believe in TAKING RISKS, following my HEART and PUSHING MYSELF
to places I never knew before.

I believe in MY ABILITIES, MY STRENGTH and MY PURPOSE.

I believe HAPPINESS comes from WITHIN.

I believe it takes COURAGE to become WHO YOU TRULY ARE
and in making my own DREAMS COME TRUE.

I believe that tomorrow is A GRAND NEW DAY.
and I truly believe ANYTHING IS POSSIBLE.

YOUR MANIFESTO

DESIGNING *for the* LORNA JANE WOMAN

FOR AS LONG AS I CAN REMEMBER I HAVE BEEN INTERESTED IN FASHION.

I was crocheting bikinis when I was 16, customising my clothing from age 18 and spending weekends when I was 21 designing and making my own clothes.

I guess you could say that my love of health and fitness, fashion and the need to create beautiful things has been the driving force for the best part of my life. I have somehow managed to take the things I love the most and build a great life and a successful business out of them.

On Design

I believe a designer should enhance the way you live by creating products for you to love and be inspired by. The active wear we create at Lorna Jane is the culmination of my years spent trying to find things that didn't exist in the marketplace and developing products I would love to have and wear in my own active life.

Designing for the Lorna Jane woman is easy for me because '*I am the Lorna Jane woman!*' I have personally spent hours in the gym, running, strength training, sweating in Bikram yoga studios, spinning on bikes and hiking on many a trail. I need great active wear that can perform when I need it to; but also make me feel athletic and super cute in my regular life.

I design products that I want to wear and my personal mantras and philosophies infiltrate all aspects of the brand, from the meaning of the three Lorna Jane icons (Move Nourish Believe) to the inspirational singlets splayed with my favourite motivational words and quotes.

From first-hand experience I know there are a lot of things women need from their active wear and I want every garment to make you feel fit, comfortable and supported. I also know that you work out to feel good but you want to look good whilst you're doing it.

I THINK TO BE A SUCCESSFUL DESIGNER YOU HAVE TO LIVE AN INSPIRATIONAL LIFE.

And I draw my inspiration from everything I do in my life: from travelling to new and unusual places, to the books I read, the movies I watch, how I work out, the people in my life. Even some of the reality TV shows I watch!

I get my best ideas – the thoughts that have really elevated my business and revolutionised Lorna Jane – when I am most relaxed and having fun. And I often use this reasoning to convince my husband that we need to go on an amazing holiday, so that we can clear our heads and do some of our best creative thinking.

Taking a break from your 'everyday' and shaking things up a little is sometimes all that is needed to clear out the cobwebs and ignite your creative thinking.

It could be as simple as taking your computer to the local coffee shop one or two mornings a week to give you a different perspective, or going for a walk at lunchtime to clear your head. Just as rituals are important to create successful lives so is spontaneity, having new experiences, enjoying life and having fun.

Over the years Lorna Jane has developed into a brand that goes beyond conventional active-wear, although it was never my original intention. But as the Founder, Dream Keeper and Creative Director sitting over all creative decisions, I guess it was only natural that my thoughts, words and philosophies in life would become those of my brand.

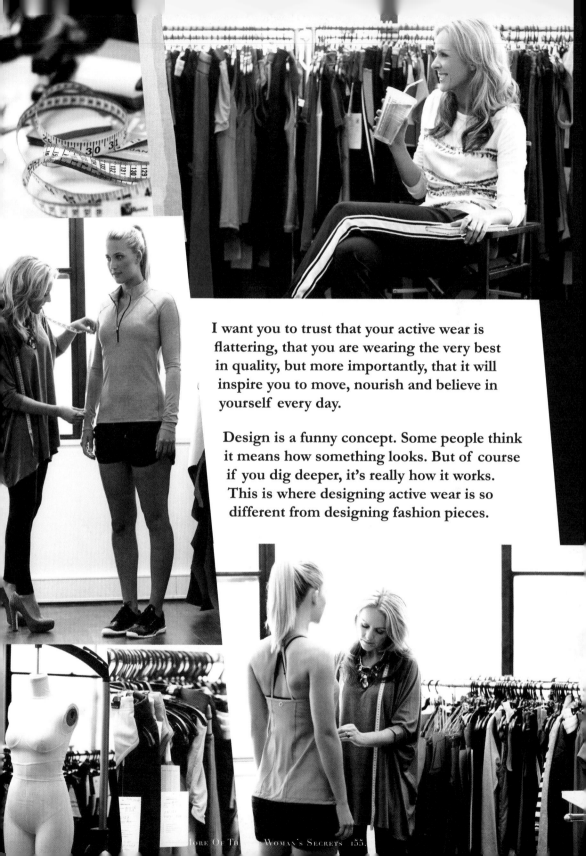

I want you to trust that your active wear is flattering, that you are wearing the very best in quality, but more importantly, that it will inspire you to move, nourish and believe in yourself every day.

Design is a funny concept. Some people think it means how something looks. But of course if you dig deeper, it's really how it works. This is where designing active wear is so different from designing fashion pieces.

In the early days I used to think I was less of a 'designer' because I wasn't creating one-off pieces for a special occasion that women would treasure for the rest of their lives. But now I realise that what I design has so much more impact on a woman's life than any fashion piece could ever have. I have the ability to inspire women towards a fitter and healthier life through my work and that motivates me to do my best work every single day.

Ultimately the pieces we design at Lorna Jane need to function first and look good second – although we like to think we do both equally as well.

To design something really well you have to 'get it'. And I know without a doubt that to design great active wear you absolutely, positively have to exercise.

All of our pieces at Lorna Jane are road-tested by our team of active people. They spend hours mimicking what our customers will do in our products – run, spin and downward dog – to make sure that you will not be disappointed. But, more importantly, to give you all those little things in a garment that you might not see when you initially buy the product but that you will appreciate when you work out in it.

I also believe that to be creative and to do your best and most inspiring work you need to not only lead an inspiring life full of everything that you love to do, but it is essential that you create a space that allows you to think, feel and be at your most creative.

For me, designing and any other form of creative thought needs isolation. I love to work with my team and throw around concepts and ideas but when it comes to putting everything down on paper I like to surround myself with all of my ideas and inspirations, work through the possibilities and come up with a plan on my own.

It may be because I started my design career being the only designer with little or no input from anyone else, who knows! But what I do know for sure is that everyone is different – some of us like to listen to music, others like to get outdoors … whatever you feel you need to do.

The most important thing here is to recognise what you have to do to produce your best, most creative work and start doing it more often so that you continue to create and innovate.

Another thing that I always do is I have a notebook handy to jot down any thoughts and ideas I might have, wherever I am. I have them in all of my handbags, in my car, at my desk both at home and at work. I even have one by the side of my bed just in case inspiration strikes in the middle of the night!

Fashion designer Tom Ford was explaining his design process and he likened it to thinking and thinking and thinking and then suddenly when it all came together, actually feeling something.

When I design I go through a similar thing because I design what I love and what I would wear myself. I will just keep thinking, changing, re-arranging, walking away for a while and so forth until it just happens. It turns into something that I want, love and can't wait to wear. I actually look at my drawing and FEEL something.

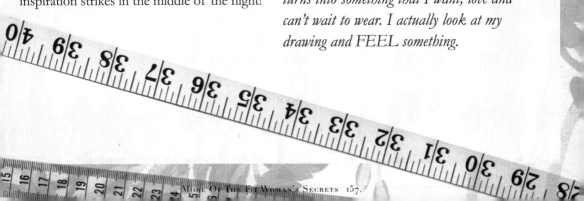

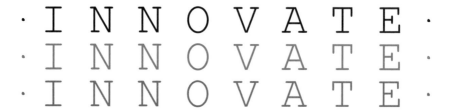

· I N N O V A T E ·
· I N N O V A T E ·
· I N N O V A T E ·

> To live a creative life we must lose
> our fear of being wrong.

TRUE INNOVATORS DRAW INSPIRATION FROM THEIR IMAGINATION – they live to challenge the commonly accepted; they see no limits and are constantly daring to make things different.

Of course, the more you innovate and refuse to accept ordinary, the more you are bound to make mistakes and that is because when it comes to innovation, failure is an essential part of the journey to success.

As a designer, one of the most important things to remember in your pursuit of innovation is that you will make mistakes and that you have to be willing to be wrong over and over again if you want to come up with something truly original.

Another challenge designers face is the fact that we are always looking for perfection *(we are never satisfied)* and I guess that's why we continuously come up with new ideas … because we are always looking to do things better.

At Lorna Jane, there are more than 20 years of design expertise in every garment but still we continue to make innovation one of the most crucial elements in the design process. We have a successful formula but we also want to give you the new! The MORE!

We are constantly innovating and inventing better ways to do things in the endless pursuit of fit fashion. We are not afraid to ask our customers how we can do things better as we understand that our customer is King – or should I say, Queen!

Every garment that makes the cut offers you innovation and motivation to get fit, a little something more to make you feel good and look great when you work out and the very latest technology and fashion-forward approach to living active.

We are an innovator in the active-wear category and are committed to giving you an active wardrobe that takes you from workout to wind-down seamlessly. We believe that if you feel confident enough to wear your active wear in your everyday life that you will actually want to exercise more often.

We also believe that it makes sense to invest in pieces that not only work for your training sessions but in your life – clothing that makes you feel just as on-trend in life as when you are working out.

Creativity is in our DNA. It's what makes our hearts beat faster and why we love what we do.

We want to give our customers all the things that they know and love about our products but we also want to surprise and delight them – give them

MORE.

DO
ALL
THINGS
WITH
LOVE

12 THINGS SUCCESSFUL PEOPLE DO DIFFERENTLY

1. They create and pursue SMART goals.

2. They take decisive and immediate ACTION.

3. They FOCUS on being productive, not being busy.

4. They make LOGICAL, informed decisions.

5. They avoid the TRAP of trying to make things perfect.

6. They work OUTSIDE of their comfort zone.

7. They keep things SIMPLE.

8. They focus on making small, continuous IMPROVEMENTS.

9. They measure and track their PROGRESS.

10. They maintain a POSITIVE outlook as they learn from mistakes.

11. They spend time with the RIGHT people.

12. They maintain BALANCE in their life.

BEHIND THE SCENES
AT LORNA JANE

I AM OFTEN ASKED WHAT HAPPENS BEHIND THE SCENES AT LORNA JANE
*and I guess the most obvious but honest answer is that we simply live and promote
the Active Living Dream. We spend 24/7 thinking, inspiring, motivating and spreading
the message of Move Nourish Believe. We are passionate about inspiring women and
doing whatever it takes to reach as many women as possible with this life-changing message.*

HERE ARE JUST A FEW OF OUR CANDID ACTIVE LIVING MOMENTS IN TIME.

Team LG – Behind the Camera

September Photoshoot Selecting

April Photoshoot in the Park

Roger Directing

With Bec – Our MNB Ambassador

Playing cover girl for Messenger
Collective Magazine

In front of the camera

Roger on location

Some of my amazing team on our December photoshoot

KODAK PORTRA 160   47   48

RUN GIRL RUN
MOVE YOUR BODY

Active Nation Day

Early days of 'MORE'... Book Planning

Roger doing what he does best!

September Beach Photoshoot

DAY IN THE LIFE

There isn't really what you could call a 'usual day' for me …
but that's exactly why I love my work and my life! Every day
I am presented with new challenges and opportunities to
improve Lorna Jane and how we go about inspiring women
to live their best active life.

I do start each morning bright and early with exercise;
either yoga, a weight session, a run or sometimes just
walking my dog. I'll then relax over a healthy breakfast while
I catch up on my emails before heading into the office.

I'm usually with the design team for the first few hours,
fitting our latest collections, selecting new fabrics or running
through upcoming trends and inspirations. You can then
typically find me in back-to-back meetings for the rest
of the day.

My afternoons are usually dedicated to meeting with our
marketing team, where we are either on location shooting
our new collections, working through our latest catalogue or
planning new campaigns. It's always a 'good day' if I can
find time to work on my current book or write for my MNB
Blog before I leave the office usually around 7pm.

I catch up with my husband whilst walking our dog, this is
followed with some yoga stretching before a relaxing dinner
at home. Then I'll either read, catch a movie or do some
work on a future project. I go to bed at about 10pm or 11pm
and fortunately I don't need a lot of sleep because I am up
again at 5am to do it all over again.

Life can be pretty CHAOTIC at times, but I know one thing for sure: each and every day will have its own set of OPPORTUNITIES and challenges and that's absolutely FINE BY ME!

day in the life

OF LORNA JANE CLARKSON

5:30AM
Hot water and lemon drink followed by 15min of stretching

6:15AM-6:30AM
Thinking time whilst I walk Roger

7:00AM
Workout

8:00AM
Breakfast

9-9.30AM
My work day begins

6:00-7:00PM
Head home for another
walk with Roger and
some yoga then dinner

DANCE **LOVE**

MNB
IS THE
NEW
BLACK

8:30PM
Lay out my workout wear and
plan the next day

9:00-10:30PM
Read, write or watch a movie

WHAT LIES AHEAD

GOING GLOBAL
- FIRST STOP CALIFORNIA

Lorna Jane has come so far. We are often surprised but always grateful for what we have achieved and where this experience has taken us.

It wasn't our plan to open as many stores in Australia as we have and it certainly wasn't our plan to take Lorna Jane global. Our expansion decisions are always driven by demand, so as we opened more and more stores in Australia and the interest from other countries started flooding in, it became increasingly obvious that 'going global' had to be the next step if we were to meet demand and continue our journey to inspire women towards Active Living.

Lorna Jane had reached a stage where we had successfully defined our message over 23 years of national expansion, we had made a name for ourselves as a quality brand, we had the confidence and the financial security of an established business and we were ready for a new challenge.

**So the question was:
where to from here?**
We put together a plan and decided that the first step forward would be to open stores in the US, starting with 25 in California. And so it began ...

If I'm completely honest, the logistics of creating products for a different season, opening stores, getting the right people on board and making sure our message to inspire women was translated correctly was a little overwhelming to say the least.

But in typical Lorna Jane fashion we just got the right people in the room, put a plan together, placed one foot in front of the other and got things moving! I clearly remember sitting in a board meeting discussing the first store opening, wondering how the hell we could possibly pull it off. Then six months later, after we had opened an additional five stores, sitting there talking about our future openings in the US as if they were happening in Adelaide or Perth. No worries!

Timing is everything – and I think having over 23 years to establish our brand in Australia and develop a strong understanding of what Lorna Jane represented in the marketplace had put us in the perfect position to take on this new challenge.

We also did a ridiculous amount of research when we were planning our expansion into the US and found that there were so many conflicting opinions as to how Lorna Jane should look there, and what modifications we should make for it to work for the American woman.

We took on a great deal of valuable information from our research but ultimately Bill and I made the decision to take our brand to California EXACTLY as it was in Australia. We had to trust our instincts, and they were telling us that the active American woman would love Lorna Jane in its original form, just as so many Australian women had before her. So we stood our ground, went against popular opinion, listened to our 'gut' - because who knew the Lorna Jane woman better than us? - crossed our fingers and went with it!

And you know what? We were right!

Of course with any new venture you need to accept that you might have to make adjustments to meet the market along the way. But I truly believed that I owed it to myself, my team and my new customers to be authentic, give them Lorna Jane as it should be, show them the brand I love and have spent 23 years perfecting and trust that they would be inspired by it just as much as we are.

It is still early days but the Lorna Jane customers in California have rewarded us by embracing everything the brand stands for and welcoming us with open arms.

We have discovered that the American and Australian Lorna Jane woman aren't that different. They both want active wear with great fit, superb quality and they want it from a brand that doesn't compromise on fashion. She wants to work out in comfort but also to know she can take her workout wear beyond the gym or yoga studio into her regular life with style.

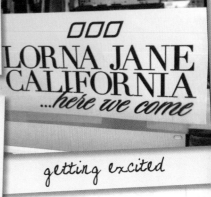

LORNA JANE
CALIFORNIA
...here we come

Mandatory LA Hike

getting excited

Venice Beach
Warehouse

team USA

the perfect backdrop

LIVING THE CALIFORNIAN DREAM - HOW DO WE DO IT?

Lorna Jane is run like a big family business and our US sister is an integral part of that family. Be careful what you wish for - we wanted a 24/7 business and now we honestly know what it feels like to have one! We are constantly talking on the phone, chatting on Skype and going back and forward with emails. We wake up in the morning to a full inbox and are constantly strategising and planning new things. But we wouldn't want it any other way!

Bill is the CEO of both companies and I creatively control everything for the US and Australia. So we are both going backwards and forwards, taking late-night calls and doing what needs to be done to make Lorna Jane US just as customer-centric, innovative and inspiring as Lorna Jane in Australia.

We started small but there's a big team in the US now and it is growing daily. We have also sent a fantastic group of Aussie girls over to California to lead the charge and ensure that the heritage and culture of Lorna Jane - what our brand truly represents - is captured in every one of our stores and every single customer experience.

We have also set up a couple of Lorna Jane 'team houses' where most of the Aussie staff live and follow the Move Nourish Believe philosophy, inspiring American women to get active. They are living 'The American Dream' and making the most of this exciting, once-in-a-lifetime experience.

We decided from the very beginning that for the US business to be a success it had to prove that it could stand alone from our Australian business as an independent start-up company. Like most small businesses there was no huge marketing budget or established customer base, so we had to go right back to the grassroots of Lorna Jane: doing trunk shows, visiting all of the local fitness centres and inviting the members into our stores.

It was just like the early days of Lorna Jane in Australia when I was teaching fitness classes and laying my outfits on the floor for women to try on after class.

We also had to make sure that we told everyone we met about the Lorna Jane story; where we started, how great our products were and the amazing philosophy of Move Nourish Believe that had inspired so many women to Active Living. We had to keep reminding ourselves and our team that we had no history in the US, we were the new kid on the block and that they had to tell as many people as they could about just how amazing Lorna Jane and the lifestyle we advocated was.

And let's not forget that we still have our Australian business to run, so I don't get to spend as much time in the US as I would like. But when I do visit I like to spend as much time with my customers and US team as humanly possible.

We have customer nights in the stores where women can come in and say hi, have a personal styling session and learn a little more about Active Living and the Move Nourish Believe philosophy.

I think one-on-one time with my customers is crucial – and that applies tenfold when you are entering into a new market. It's important that my customers have the opportunity to meet me but also that I get to spend time with them, ask them questions and listen to their feedback. It is also one of my all-time favourite things to do and a constant source of inspiration for me!

We also have a fantastic Ambassador Program in the US, with a heap of inspiring and influential fitness instructors and industry leaders wearing and endorsing our brand whilst they work out every day. This is also mimicking what I did in the early days. My friends and I wore Lorna Jane to our fitness classes and then told everyone about the products. When the class was finished, we invited them to their nearest Lorna Jane store.

Having stores in the US, and especially in LA, has also given us fantastic exposure in local and international magazines with so many celebrities wearing our products, being photographed and seen out and about in Lorna Jane. This not only benefits our US operation but the Australian business, too.

In the first year we opened 10 stores – which was more than we actually expected – and have a further 15 to open in 2013. The plan from there is to expand into other states one at a time and continue to grow and expand our US online business and social media community.

We are working really hard and I have to admit things can get a little crazy but we're enjoying every minute of it and are just grateful every day that our US expansion is proving to be a success. I guess you could say we are living our very own American dream, one Lorna Jane customer at a time!

the dream to keep inspiring women

Bill and I came to realise quite a few years ago that inspiring women to live active lives with our Move Nourish Believe philosophy was not something we could do for a few years and then move on to something else.

Inspiring women to reach their full potential, do great things and live an active and meaningful life is our quest, our passion in life and the reason we exist.

We are not happy to simply spread our message across Australia or even the US. We want to take our passion for Active Living and shout it across every corner of the world and inspire as many women as we can.

So the plan is to continue to forge forward into other counties with Lorna Jane and all it represents once we've made good inroads into the American market. We have already seen some clear interest in Canada, the UK, Hong Kong and Dubai, just to name a few.

Our plans for Lorna Jane are what we think about first thing in the morning and are quite often the last thing we talk about at night. So to say it is all-consuming, that we are a little obsessed with the global plan and how we are going to do it and do it well, is an understatement!

But we love what we do and we actually feel privileged to have this opportunity. It is so rewarding to share our personal passion with other people and to have an overwhelmingly positive response in return. I can think of no better use of my time or better way to live my life.

I am often asked when will Lorna Jane be big enough and why I continue to work so hard when I obviously have a successful business I can be proud of. The answer is simple. I love what I do.

I have discovered a way of life that truly inspires me and I have an irresistible passion to spread this message of Active Living to as many women possible.

So, for as long as women anywhere in the world will listen, respond and buy Lorna Jane,
I will continue to give my 100 per cent commitment to the design and development of our
amazing products and the promotion of Active Living and the wonderful world
it can open up for so many women.

ANYTHING
is possible

Everything I have achieved in my life, and will continue to achieve is living proof of what can happen if you truly believe anything is possible and are willing to put in the hard work to make it happen. I believe that you have a gift that only you can give to the world, it is the reason you are here and you owe it to yourself to follow your heart, pursue your dreams, take chances and believe in yourself.

Always remember that a positive mindset and belief in yourself and your ability to achieve great things is the beginning of all the good things that happen in your life. Dare to dream because with a little hard work and determination you can honestly create the life you have always imagined.

Believing anything is possible really boils down to confidence. This doesn't mean you have to look like you've got it totally together all the time or are supremely self-assured. And trust me when I tell you that confidence isn't always about the external; it comes from how we're feeling within.

So many of us lack confidence, but with practice
you can learn to master it.

Here are a few tips:

The more you smile or laugh, literally the happier - and more confident and relaxed - you'll feel. **SMILING AND LAUGHING** releases a chemical in your brain that heightens your mood, and they also make you look far more inviting to other people and consequently invite good things into your life.

EVERYONE MAKES MISTAKES and if your mistakes are in the past, that's exactly where they belong - let them go. How can you be happy and confident when you are living in a state of fear, anxiety or regret?

HONOUR THE LIFESTYLE AND BLESSINGS YOU HAVE. While it's healthy to strive for more, if you simmer in resentment because you perceive you don't have enough or others have it better than you, you will never grow and achieve. Or be confident.

If someone has hurt or betrayed you, ignored or overlooked you, learn to forgive if not forget. To hang on to anger, pain, anguish and sorrow is only hurting you, not them. It will also eat away at your happiness and confidence until there is nothing left. **FORGIVENESS** can be hard at first, but it is so liberating that you'll never hold on to hurt feelings again.

Take on new **CHALLENGES** that test you. When you do something a little out of your comfort zone and run with it, the natural boost of confidence and euphoria it gives you is truly amazing and quite possibly addictive.

Instead of beating yourself up all the time, write a list of 10 good points about yourself and add one more good point to the list each day. Every day read the list of good points and learn to **CELEBRATE THE THINGS YOU LOVE ABOUT YOURSELF**. Trust me, this makes you instantly feel good about yourself and boosts your confidence over time.

There's no escaping the fact that things in life happen from time to time to knock your confidence and rob you of your greatness and purpose. Make the decision to resist succumbing to feelings of hopelessness and defeat. Ups and downs are an entirely normal part of life. It is all about how you **HANDLE THE SITUATION** and what you learn from it that counts.

Confidence is a natural state that we should celebrate and enjoy – you just have to watch a young child to realise that! **THERE REALLY ISN'T ANYTHING MORE ATTRACTIVE THAN A WOMAN WHO IS QUIETLY CONFIDENT IN HER OWN SKIN**, content with where her life is heading and making the most of the opportunities each day brings her way.

SO LET'S TAKE IT UPON OURSELVES TO BE THAT WOMAN – SHINE IN OUR OWN CONFIDENCE AND CELEBRATE OUR LIVES, EVERYTHING AND EVERYONE IN THEM AND THE BRIGHT AND PROMISING FUTURE WE ARE CREATING FOR OURSELVES.

WHY
I WILL
DO THIS
FOREVER

I will advocate Active Living for as long as I possibly can. Lorna Jane and inspiring women towards Active Living with my MNB philosophy isn't just a job for me. It isn't something I could stop doing and, quite frankly, there isn't anything I would rather spend my time doing. It is what I love and right now I can see myself doing it forever.

Would you ask an environmental campaigner or an animal activist when they were going to walk away from their passion, pack it all in and go lie on a remote beach and forget about everything they had been spending the first part of their lives fighting for? I don't think so! So why would I do it when my motivation is the same?

I am not inspired by building personal wealth, but by my dream to inspire and educate people on the benefits and enjoyment that come from living a bigger and more authentic life, being fit and healthy and following their dreams. And honestly, when you look at the health and obesity statistics, suicide rates and the general state of the economies both here and overseas, I have so much more work to do.

WHY ARE WE FOCUSING ON WOMEN? Because it is my belief that women play one of the most powerful roles in the family unit. It is the woman who decides what her family eats, what activities they do, how much sport her children play, how much television the kids get to watch ... and the list goes on and on.

I WANT TO CHANGE THE WAY THE WORLD IS HEADING. I want to inspire women to reach their full potential in life and to teach their children to think and do the same. I want to teach them how living an Active Life will ultimately give them more energy and enthusiasm for everything else in their lives and that it's only when they start to believe anything is possible, that their dreams will start to come true.

IF LORNA JANE CAN INSPIRE just one woman to live an active life with our Move Nourish Believe philosophy, and teach to put her and her family's health first, then hopefully we can inspire many more families, a community and maybe, just maybe, even a city or an entire country.

AS I OFTEN SAY
TO MY TEAM:

*"We are an army of Active
Women attempting to change
the world ... one Lorna Jane
customer at a time."*

WHO *inspires* ME?

I am constantly asked who inspires me – and the answer is YOU – the women who read my books, wear my products and follow my Move Nourish Believe philosophy. When I answer this question, I am not 100 per cent sure that people believe me but I promise it's the total, honest truth.

Pretty much everything I do is driven by the love I have for my customers. I am inspired by their response to what I do, how it motivates them to think and be more active, and how what we do has changed their lives and given them more confidence to achieve great things. I feel incredibly blessed to influence people's lives in the small way that I do and I thank you from the bottom of my heart. Knowing that you love what we do inspires me to keep writing, designing, innovating and coming up with new ways to inspire you in your Active Life.

Another constant source of inspiration in my life is my husband Bill. Through his own actions and the many profound and unusual statements he makes, he has taught me to think bigger and fear nothing.

He can clearly see Lorna Jane as a global company and gives me encouragement and guidance every single day to reach higher and achieve more. He is also my wing-man, my Robin, my partner in life: and I know he will always be there by my side through the good times and the bad, making this journey so much more of a celebration than I ever would have imagined.

My Mum has also been a huge influence in my life. She has always been my Number One Fan and encouraged me from an early age to believe in myself and strive to be and do better. She has also taught me from her own actions not to settle for second best in life, to follow your dreams and to work hard to make things happen.

WE ARE
SO GOOD
TOGETHER

Q & A *with*
BILL CLARKSON

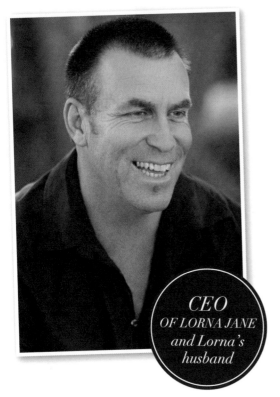

CEO OF LORNA JANE and Lorna's husband

How does Lorna make you a better person?
Because she sweats the details.

If you were to suggest an actress to play Lorna in a film, who would you say?
Lorna is a hard act to follow ... but maybe Jennifer Aniston.

3 words to describe Lorna?
... The REAL DEAL! You said 3 words?!

What do you LOVE about Lorna?
Everything. (And I'm not just saying that because I know she will be reading this!).

How does she take her coffee?
A long black.

Describe your perfect day together?
Beach walk. Coffee @ Costa. Breakfast at home. Lunch with friends. Relaxing afternoon reading. Dinner at home and an early night.

Your favourite outfit she wears?
Has to be anything LJ of course!

Your finest, most favourite memory of your relationship?
Our wedding day!

One thing Lorna wouldn't know you think about her?
Lorna makes me want to be a better person!

When did you realise you LOVED her?
The first time I met her I said to the guy I was standing with, "I will marry that girl one day!"

What would you say is the secret to keeping your relationship alive?
Understanding the bigger picture!

What would you say is Lorna's most annoying habit? (be careful, she's reading!!!)
She's a perfectionist!

The best gift you've even been given by Lorna? And vice versa?
My fav gift from Lorna would be the Mini Moke she gave me for Christmas 2012, and I think Lorna would say her fav gift from me would be Roger our puppy ... who I think would be our fav gift EVER!

How are you the Ying to Lorna's Yang (in a business sense)?
I'm the bigger thinker, she is the perfectionist!

What was life like before Lorna Jane?
Underachieving!

Who do you consider to be the biggest living legend?
Wow, big question...If you asked me 18 months ago, Steve Jobs would have been my pick! Now I'm not sure, so you'll have to ask me in another 5 years!

Which talent would you most like to have?

Experience says you can't be great at everything. I am happy with the talents I have, I just need to practise more.

If you could change one thing about yourself what would it be?

Expecting other people to think like me. Sometimes I think I was born on another planet.

Which words or phrases do you most overuse?

Think differently!

Your best ever business analogy?

God gave us two ears and just one mouth... for the simple reason that we should spend MORE time listening.

Dream person to have a business lunch with and why?

Every time I meet a 'supposedly great person' I come away disappointed. Give me lunch with Lorna and Roger any day!

QUIRKY QUESTIONS

If you owned your own restaurant, what would it be called?

Nourish.

Your favourite T-Shirt and why?

V-neck. The thinner the better!

Favourite band of all time?

Eagles – shows my age!

Bedside book of the moment?

Purple Cow – Simon Sinek.

Favourite place to holiday in the world?

Sunrise Beach, QLD.

Favourite place to eat in LA?

True Foods, Santa Monica.

Your ultimate workout?

A game of touch footy.

If you could be a superhero, what would your powers be?

To change people's minds and the way they think!

If you could have a conversation with someone from history who would it be?

Steve Jobs without a doubt!

If you had a 60 second Super Bowl advertisement what would you want to show a billion people?

ACTIVE LIVING, and the difference it can make.

If you had an extra hour every day what would you do with it?

Think more.

PERSONAL QUESTIONS

Proudest success?

CEO of the year 2012.

Who are your heroes in real life?

Anyone that has a go!

Describe your perfect day?

Tomorrow.

If you could retire right now, would you?

No, why would I?

What 3 adjectives would you use to describe your life?

On my tombstone – here lies a man that left no stone unturned.

A book you would read then re-read again?

I have never read a book twice, never will!

If you could have dinner with 5 people living or dead who would they be?

My wife - Lorna. Steve Jobs - Visionary. My childhood friend - Chris Neilson (talk about the old days). Mickey Drexler - CEO of J.Crew and revolutionary retailer. Jamie Oliver - Food!

5 things ABOUT BILL

... Coffee or tea? **Tea**
... Beach or mountains? **Beach**
... Football or cricket? **Football**
... Business mantra? **Never Give Up**
... Morning or night? **Morning**

BETWEEN
you and me

Stories are what make people and brands come alive. They define us, they create intrigue and a sense of mystery. They are the emotional glue that connects us to the people, places and events that become our most treasured memories.

I love hearing people's stories and I truly believe that they give an amazing insight into who we are and what we stand for in life.

Because of this, and also because there are few questions that I am often asked about myself and my business, I thought I would share with you some of my stories, the ones you might not know about me or about Lorna Jane and others that will dispel any rumours and set the record straight.

There is nothing better than having the opportunity to share experiences and I hope my stories give you a little more insight into my life, the life of Lorna Jane, everything we stand for and believe in, as well as some of the interesting and funny things that happened to us along the way.

"Lorna Jane original logo 1989"

Why I called my brand Lorna Jane.

Often when I meet people for the first time they get a little confused with my name! They'll ask should they call me Lorna, Lorna Jane or Ms Clarkson. Is my name Lorna Jane or is it Lorna Jane Clarkson?

Even funnier still, Bill (my husband) has been referred to on more than just a few occasions as Bill Jane instead of Bill Clarkson!

I thought by naming my brand after myself it would have made it simple but obviously that is not the case! The reason I use my first and middle name also has a little story behind it.

When I was teaching fitness classes and way before Lorna Jane, there were two Lornas on the aerobic timetable and the gym needed to make it clear which one of us was teaching. So I suggested using my middle name to differentiate my classes from hers ... and that's when people started calling me Lorna Jane.

The reason I decided to use my name as the name of my active-wear label was to signify my personal commitment to the fit, quality and design of each and every piece. If you look at our very first logo, you will see that it looks like my signature and I did that because I wanted to symbolise me signing off and approving each garment. I guess you could say I was giving it my personal guarantee.

Why Lorna Jane is women's only.

I knew from the day I decided to start my own active-wear brand that it would be for women only. I was really passionate about designing for women and to be totally honest, menswear just didn't interest me.

Another key reason is that women play such a powerful role in the family unit and my aim is to inspire and motivate one active woman at a time through Lorna Jane until everyone around the world is living their best life through Active Living.

I also wanted to create the sort of environment in our stores that was feminine and inspirational to women. When I started my business there were already so many male-dominated sports stores in the marketplace so I wanted to offer something different; a place where women could come to buy their active wear but also share recipes, plan workouts together and make friends with other active women.

I also can't really imagine a man wearing a brand called Lorna Jane … Can you?

Why we pay the price for quality.

When I decided to make active-wear and guarantee the quality by putting my name on it, I made a promise to myself and to my customers that I would always give them the very best in workmanship, fit and function.

It is important to me that you get the very best technology, that your active wear makes exercising more enjoyable because it performs for you, and that you can wear your Lorna Jane pieces day in and day out, through the most rigorous of workouts without them fading, pilling or going out of shape.

When you buy Lorna Jane you know that you are investing in quality. So when I read on Instagram and Facebook that some people love Lorna Jane and want to buy more but wish it could be cheaper; my answer is simple: I wish I could give it to you at a cheaper price because then more people would wear it. But the simple fact is, real quality costs more to produce.

At Lorna Jane our fabric is trademarked technology from the best mills in the world, it has a flattering matt finish and is woven so tight that you can squat with confidence knowing that you won't ever be over-exposed.

We have the very best team of designers and technicians who make sure every style goes through a rigorous sampling and fitting procedure, followed by extensive washing and workout testing.

We put in the time, we put in the technology and we use our extensive knowledge and skill so we can guarantee that what you receive is a superior, intelligent product that enhances your workout experience and inspires you to live an active life.

Would we like to do all of this and give it to you at a cheaper price? Absolutely! But it would have to come at a cost to quality and we know that you wouldn't want us to compromise on anything to do with the amazing products that you know and love.

What our three icons represent:

Our three icons have been an integral part of the Lorna Jane brand pretty much from Day 1.

They were first developed as a single icon, created by linking the L and the J of Lorna Jane to form a slightly off-kilter square.

We used the single icon for the first couple of years but the reason we now have three is because I wanted the icons to represent my personal philosophy of Move Nourish Believe, and I thought that if I put the three icons on my active wear it would inspire the women who wore the product to:

Move their bodies every day
Nourish from the inside out
And Believe anything is possible

And you know what; I think it works! Customers tell me all the time that Lorna Jane products inspire them in their active lives – which is even more evidence that if you believe, I mean really believe in something it really can come true.

Where our catch-cry of 'NEVER NEVER NEVER GIVE UP' came from

We were in the process of building our first fitness centre. Construction was running a couple of weeks behind schedule, finances were getting a little low and, to top things off, Lorna Jane was going through a huge growth stage. So to say we were under a little pressure was an understatement!

On one of the half-finished walls of the gym I hung a really cute cartoon image of a frog who demonstrated extreme optimism when faced with a huge challenge, with the words Never Give Up underneath.

It really resonated with me and I thought it would also resonate with our staff at the time so I added a few more 'Nevers' and printed it on a singlet. The rest is history!

I didn't know it at the time but those motivational words were what we needed to push through the growth challenges at Lorna Jane. Because of this they have become an integral part of what our brand represents. They inspire our customers to overcome obstacles in their own lives. I have seen them worn on TV when people have been cleaning up after the devastation of floods and cyclones. I have seen them represent hope after debilitating accidents and help people through their recovery. And I have seen them simply motivate you to get through that workout when you really didn't feel like exercising but you pushed yourself to do it anyway.

At Lorna Jane our inspirational messages are an integral part of our brand DNA and we have so many that we love to share with you.

But Never Never Never Give Up is the one that truly represents what our brand is all about. It is cemented in our history and will be an important part of our brand for as long as it continues to inspire you.

Why wearing Lorna Jane really does make you want to exercise MORE

I am often told by my customers that there must be a secret ingredient in the Lorna Jane products because when they wear them they actually feel like exercising MORE. They feel like they want to train harder, and they want to be healthier and have more fun!

One possible explanation could be that Lorna Jane makes you look good and I know for sure that when you look good, you feel good. But there is one other answer that I'd like to share with you for the almost magical effect Lorna Jane has on people.

For some time now we have been making sure that there is a little bit of love injected into each and every garment. Literally.

As our business grew, Bill and I wanted to instill in our team the importance of putting love into everything they did at Lorna Jane. Just as food tastes better when it is prepared with love, we believe if we inject a little love into all of our products then our customers will feel our commitment and passion towards inspiring them to live their best, most active life when they wear Lorna Jane.

So we started to attach small heart-shaped beads into our products (some are visible whilst others are harder to find) with the understanding that our team designing, sewing and constructing our garments give their love and passion for Active Living and infuse it into every piece.

The heart bead is our symbol, our secret ingredient if you like, that will pass this passion on to our customers when they wear Lorna Jane, inspiring them to Move Nourish and Believe in themselves every day.

These hearts are not designed to stay in your Lorna Jane products for the life of the garment – but just long enough that you feel the benefit and develop your own inspiration and motivation to be fit and healthy.

This is the first time I have actually spoken about this and I know I run the risk of you thinking I am a little crazy - but how else can I explain the way Lorna Jane makes so many people feel good, except that …we make it with love.

How we almost lost Bill.

It was just after the GFC hit and retail was going through a difficult time. At Lorna Jane we were making the most of the fact that most businesses were slowing down their expansion and we were growing and actually doing really well because of it.

My husband Bill is the CEO of the company and he got a phone call one morning from one of Australia's leading retail companies at the time, offering him a great deal of money to jump ship, leave Lorna Jane and join their brand.

Understanding that they obviously didn't know he was my husband and partner in Lorna Jane, Bill politely turned them down by saying:
"I don't think my wife would want me to leave Lorna Jane!"

I have often wondered if at a later date they realised their oversight and had a little chuckle to themselves, as we all did at Lorna Jane.

How Move Nourish Believe became inseparable from Lorna Jane.

MNB has been my personal philosophy for as long as I can remember and I had never thought to make it part of the Lorna Jane brand until my customers started asking me how I managed to stay so fit and healthy and run a successful business at the same time.

We had decided to do a campaign on the woman behind the brand and called it Move Nourish Believe. When we released the campaign I did a national tour of the stores to meet customers and connect with my team and was asked over and over again when I was going to write a book.
I hadn't really contemplated writing a book before and to be quite honest I really didn't think I had achieved enough that anyone would want to read about! But when I finished the tour, I sat down with my team and we asked our customers through Facebook what they would like me to write about.

Within an hour of posting the question there was an overwhelming number of responses asking what I ate, how often I exercised, how I managed to stay motivated to exercise and run a business at the same time, and so on.

So then pressured by my team and to answer all of your questions, I decided to write a book about my philosophy for living a healthy and active life based on the Move Nourish Believe philosophy and the icons of the Lorna Jane brand. I had been living and talking about this philosophy and the concept of Active Living for quite a few years before I wrote the book – but it was only when I had the opportunity to explain it in such detail that my customers started to adopt it into their own lives and it became inseparable from Lorna Jane.

When we knew we were truly onto something

We had just opened our first real Lorna Jane store (by real, I mean independent of a fitness centre) and I was designing and cutting the garments with one other staff member under our house. Bill was looking after the accounts and splitting the hours in-store with me.

This particular day Bill was working the store and I was busy with orders. It was about 2pm and to my surprise Bill arrived home early. My initial reaction was to ask him if there was anything wrong and then to ask who was looking after the store.

He just looked at me with a silly grin on his face and said: "I had to close the store because I actually sold EVERYTHING!" At first I thought he was joking but after he explained that a woman from Singapore had come in and purchased absolutely everything we had in stock – and then showed me the money to prove it – I spent the next few minutes laughing and screaming and hugging everyone in sight.

I had to close the store because I actually sold EVERYTHING!

It was such an amazing feeling to think that someone loved what we did so much that they would buy it ALL. I only got to celebrate for a millisecond because I suddenly realised that to re-open the store we actually needed more stock.

So I put my head down and spent the next few days (and nights) designing and cutting and sewing so we could keep trading – all the time thinking 'You know what, if someone can come in to the store and love Lorna Jane enough to buy everything then we really must be onto something!'

50 WAYS
— TO —
MNB

Active Living is a way of life that allows you to think, be and perform at your best – and my Move Nourish Believe philosophy are the tools that help you achieve it.

We have put together 50 ways to Move Nourish and Believe to inspire you on your Active Living journey.

ENJOY!

Lx

Move

1. **RISE AND SHINE, IT'S TIME TO CLOCK IN SOME MOVE TIME.** Working out in the AM is a great way to set your intention for the day, clear your mind and boost your metabolism for an active day ahead.

2. **KEEP IT SIMPLE. DO WHAT YOU CAN, WHEN YOU CAN.** You don't need all the bells and whistles to have a quality workout.

3. **MIX UP YOUR ROUTINE.** Your body gets used to doing the same exercise all the time, so if you're a frequent flyer at spin class, why not challenge yourself with an hour of cross-fit instead.

4. **LISTEN TO YOUR BODY BECAUSE IT IS ONE SMART COOKIE.** If you really tune in, it will tell you important things like when you're tired, hungry, stressed or sick.

5. **THE BEAUTY OF YOGA IS MANIFOLD.** Not only does regular yoga practice hold many physical benefits such as improvement in muscle tone and strength, as well as better posture, it also brings a harmonious balance to the mind, body and spirit through the poses, controlled breathing and meditation.

6. **TURN OFF THE TV.** Research shows that those who cut their viewing time in half burn up to 120 more calories per day. It is also a nice vacation for the mind.

7. **WATCH YOUR TECHNIQUE WHEN RUNNING.** Run tall and open your chest, rather than leaning forward. This will lessen the pressure on your lower back and knees.

8. **DO PILATES TO STRENGTHEN YOUR CORE.** It will make your body more resilient to injuries and improve your posture so you look leaner and taller.

9. **FIND YOURSELF A SPORTY SISTER TO WORKOUT WITH.** It will make the hard work much more fun and you will push yourself just that little bit harder.

10. **DOWNLOAD A 50-MINUTE MUSIC PLAYLIST, AND DON'T STOP UNTIL IT STOPS.** Music is a great way to keep you amped and ready to clock up some move time.

11. **STRENGTH TRAINING ACTUALLY BURNS MORE FAT** than cardio because of the amount of calories burnt after a weight training session. Studies have shown that after a weights session your metabolism increases for up to 48 hours – now that's an incentive to start working weights into your regime!

12. **WHEN YOU ARE BUSY CLEANING THE HOUSE, TURN IT INTO A WORKOUT!** Use it as an excuse to do a wall squat, churn out a few walking lunges and really put your back into mopping that floor.

13. **BE PREPARED.** Lay out your active wear the night before so you have no excuses in the morning

14. **DON'T SKIP SQUATS:** they burn more calories per rep than almost any other move. But make sure you do them properly!

15. **AMP UP YOUR INCIDENTAL EXERCISE.** Get off the bus one stop earlier or park your car further away from your destination. It all counts, ladies!

16. **A ONE-HOUR WORKOUT IS ONLY 4% OF YOUR DAY – SO NO EXCUSES.**

17. **EVERY DAY IS A GOOD DAY TO WORKOUT!**

18. **THE HARDEST THING ABOUT EXERCISE** is to start doing it; once you are doing exercise regularly, the hardest thing to do is stop.

19. **RUNNING CAN BE A PAIN IN THE BUTT,** but it can sure give you a good one.

20. **TO SWEAT MEANS YOU ARE DETERMINED, PASSIONATE, FEARLESS AND UNSTOPPABLE.** So don't be afraid to break a sweat.

21. **INCREASING LEAN MUSCLE TISSUE** helps you burn more calories.

22. **HAVE AT LEAST ONE TO TWO REST DAYS PER WEEK.** This will allow your muscles to recover and will stop any fatigue.

23. **IF YOU HAVE A DESK JOB,** make sure you have an ergonomic chair and desk setup, and always make time to move. Stand up, move your legs and stretch every 15 minutes. You will be grateful you did in 20 years' time.

24. **STRETCH EVERY DAY** – first thing in the morning and/ or last thing at night.

25. **IF YOU HAVE ONLY 15 MINUTES TO EXERCISE** don't use it as an excuse. 15 minutes is better than nothing!

26. **RELISH ANY MOMENT TO BUST A MOVE, AND HAVE A DANCE!**

27. **RUN AROUND AFTER YOUR KIDS MORE.** Not only will it make their day, it can be a great workout too!

28. **EXPERIMENT WITH NEW AND EXCITING WORKOUTS** that are a little out of your comfort zone. Trapeze, rock climbing and cross-fit are all fun and exciting options.

29. **RIDE YOUR BIKE!**

30. **WORK ON YOUR CORE.** It will help reduce back pain and other body ailments. Practise with planks and see how many minutes you can hold the position.

31. **THERE IS TRUTH IN THE SAYING, "WHEN YOU LOOK GOOD, YOU FEEL GOOD."** An active lifestyle promotes confidence, energy and vitality.

32. **DEPENDING ON YOUR WEIGHT AND INTENSITY,** you can burn between 70 and 110 extra calories in a 10 minute workout – how good is that!

33. **WHILE ON HOLIDAYS,** it's important to shift your headspace and make exercise part of your holiday, even if it means getting up before everyone else, going hiking with the entire family or playing a game of cricket on the beach.

34. **USE YOUR IPHONE TO MOTIVATE YOU TO WORKOUT.** Discover new running routes and download the LJ iPhone app to keep you on track.

35. **KEEP A FITNESS JOURNAL;** it is a great tool to help you achieve results.

36. **PLAN YOUR WORKOUTS ON THE WEEKENDS** so you are all set for an active week ahead.

37. **TRY YOUR HAND AT TABATA.** This includes 20 seconds of maximum effort followed by just 10 seconds of rest for a total of seven to eight intervals.

38. **ONLINE WORKOUTS** are a great way to fit in some move time. Find a podcast or video to follow in the comfort of your own home.

39. **STRETCH IT OUT.** Roll out a mat in a sunny spot along with any props like a foam roller.

40. **DON'T JUST EXERCISE TO LOSE WEIGHT** – exercise to have fun, exude confidence and gain a heap of energy.

41. **MAKE MOVING PART OF YOUR EVERYDAY EXISTENCE.** Instead of meeting up with your friends for a coffee, meet them to go for a 5km walk.

42. **HAVE YOU EVER TRIED A WEIGHTED HULA-HOOP?** It is so much fun and really works your whole body.

43. **HAVING A BAD DAY?** Grab yourself some boxing gloves and get rid of your stress the healthy way.

44. **EVERY DAY IS A GOOD DAY TO WORKOUT.**

45. **SET YOURSELF MINI CHALLENGES** and try to beat your personal best every session.

46. **FOCUS ON SPEED AND POWER** in your next move session with Plyometrics training.

47. **CHALLENGE YOUR FRIEND OR CO-WORKER TO A PUSH-UP CHALLENGE.** It will tone your arms and help kick the three-thirtyitis.

48. **BE COURAGEOUS AND SIGN YOURSELF UP FOR A MARATHON.** This is a great goal to work towards, and an even better feeling when you cross the finish line!

49. **HIRE A PT** and create a fitness group amongst your circle of friends. This will give you an extra motivation boost, and you can rely on your sporty sisters to support you every step of the way.

50. **MOVE WITH THE SEASONS.** Embrace every seasonal change with a new move! Bikram yoga for winter and paddleboarding in summer!

Nourish

1. **FIND SOMEPLACE BEAUTIFUL TO GET LOST.**

2. **MAKE TIME FOR YOURSELF.** Take at least half an hour every day just to be you.

3. **DRINK WARM WATER AND LEMON IN THE AM.** It is proven to aid digestion, support immune function and detoxify the liver.

4. **LEARN TO SAY "NO".** When life gets super busy, have the discipline to just focus on your priorities and be willing to say "no" to everything else. This way you are identifying your values and aligning your life around what is truly important to you.

5. **AVOID FOODS CONTAINING INGREDIENTS YOU CANNOT PRONOUNCE.**

6. **CREATE AN UPLIFTING PLAYLIST** to have on repeat when you're having a bad day.

7. **EAT ONLY FOODS THAT ARE FRESH AND PERISHABLE.**

8. **STOP OVER-SCHEDULING AND OVER-COMMITTING.** Take stock and start eliminating what's really not important. Life is too precious to let it pass in a blur of unimportant obligations.

9. **TRY TO BUY YOUR MEAT ORGANICALLY** or make friends with your local butcher that way you know where it's coming from.

10. **ONE OF MY FAVOURITE QUOTES IS: "THE EARTH LAUGHS IN FLOWERS."** Take time to incorporate edible blooms like nasturtium into your salad. These simple, beautiful gifts of nature can make a huge difference to your mood and day.

11. **TURMERIC IS A CANCER KICKING,** inflammation fighting and health promoting spice. Use it in your cooking today!

12. **IF YOU HAVE A SWEET TOOTH,** stick with naturally occurring sugars, nothing artificial!

13. **STEER CLEAR OF TEMPTATION WHEN GROCERY SHOPPING AND AVOID THE CENTRE AISLES.**

14. **JUST ANOTHER REASON TO ENJOY CHOCOLATE.** Cacao and dark chocolate contains tryptophan, which helps boost your sense of wellbeing and reduce stress.

15. **EAT MORE DARK LEAFY VEGETABLES.** They contain an important vitamin called folate, a deficiency of which is linked to depression. It also contains loads of iron, which helps stabilise your mood and gives you energy.

16. **GRASS-FED MEAT** contains higher levels of iron and Omega 3 fatty acids than grain-fed meat. Omega 3s are necessary for cell function and to make mood-enhancing hormones.

17. **TRY QUINOA:** It's a complete protein and contains all the essential amino acids (the building blocks of protein) that we cannot [produce in our bodies] ourselves.

18. **ADD KALE TO YOUR NEXT SALAD.** It has the highest beta-carotene content (a potent antioxidant) of all vegetables.

19. **REMEMBER THAT FAT AIDS THE DIGESTION OF PROTEIN** - allowing you to access more of the nutrients and amino acids locked in your food - so don't eliminate it from your diet!

20. **EAT MORE CHOCOLATE, BEETROOT AND WALNUTS.** They are fantastic mood enhances and who doesn't want to be happy!

21. **ADD SOME DANDELION LEAVES TO YOUR SALAD.** It is extremely nutritious and contains 3x more potassium than bananas!

22. **DID YOU KNOW THAT SATURATED FATS ARE ACTUALLY THE MOST EASILY DIGESTED OF ALL THE FATS AND LESS LIKELY TO ACCUMULATE IN YOUR BODY?**

23. **REMEMBER TO ALWAYS FERMENT, SOAK OR SPROUT YOUR GRAINS** and legumes for easy digestion.

24. **FOR DETOXIFICATION** and to support your liver eat turmeric, mung beans and beetroot.

25. **GOOD QUALITY SLEEP** is a must for your overall health and wellbeing so it is important to develop a healthy night time routine.

26. **TRY SWITCHING OFF** and being present with a technology free weekend. No phones, no laptop and no emails!

27. **EMBRACE NATURAL AROMATHERAPIES BEFORE BED.** Try soothing essences like chamomile, neroli, rose, ylang ylang, vanilla, frankincense and clary sage.

28. **NOURISH YOUR RELATIONSHIPS.** Make time for people you care about and who bring out the best in you.

29. **KEEP THINGS OLD SCHOOL.** Write a handwritten letter and post it in the mail. Imagine the joy the person will get on the receiving end.

30. **H20 IS THE WAY TO GO.** Keeping hydrated will ensure your appetite is satiated.

31. **LAUGHING OUT LOUD CAN REDUCE CORTISOL LEVELS WITHIN THE BODY AND THEREFORE DECREASE STRESS LEVELS!**

32. **PREPARATION IS THE KEY.** Plan your meals on a Sunday to ensure you have a whole week of wholesome meals to nourish you throughout the week.

33. **ALWAYS NOURISH POST-WORKOUT.** Your body will automatically use the calories you eat for good (repair and recovery) and not bad (fat storage).

34. **COCONUT WATER IS NATURE'S NATURAL ISOTONIC HYDRATOR!** With its high electrolyte content, it will naturally rehydrate you more effectively than any other liquid.

35. **GREEN JUICING IS A SPEEDY, FAST AND NUTRITIOUS WAY** to nourish your insides quick!

36. **LOCAL IS LOVELY.** Shop at the Farmers' Market for the best in fresh produce. It is a great money saver too!

37. **BUY FRESH FLOWERS** to put beside your bed, light a scented candle and immerse yourself in a riveting read.

38. **CHIA SEEDS** are the richest plant based source of Omega 3, dietary fibre, protein and antioxidants. Sprinkle them in your smoothies, or as a salad topper!

39. **HAVE A HEALTHY BAKING DAY WITH YOUR GIRLFRIENDS!** Did anyone say healthy banana bread? Yum!

40. **STORE NUTS IN THE FREEZER.** This will stop them from going rancid, keep their omega 3 fatty acid content intact and ensure they stay as fresh as possible.

41. **WE DON'T BELIEVE IN THE WORD DIET.** We believe in eating a balance of whole, local and healthful nourishment.

42. **TREAT YOURSELF TO AN INDULGENT MASSAGE** or facial and nourish your body's largest organ, the skin!

43. **LATHER YOUR BODY IN COCONUT OIL TO MOISTURISE,** it will replenish your skin cells, improve collagen synthesis and make your skin feel like smooth silk.

44. **MAKE BODY BRUSHING PART OF YOUR EVERY DAY ROUTINE.** It is an excellent exfoliation tool, removing dead cells from the surface of the skin, allowing for cell renewal.

45. **EXPAND YOUR HORIZONS, IN EVERY WAY!**

46. **SEND A RANDOM MESSAGE TO YOUR SPORTY SISTERS** to let them know they rock. It will bring a smile to your face & theirs too.

47. **DRINK MORE HERBAL TEA.** Green tea is full of free radical scavengers (our great friend and powerful antioxidant), peppermint and chamomile are great for your digestion acting as a carminative and lavender can help you with overall relaxation.

48. **FOR BETTER DIGESTION,** eat when you are the least stressed and around those that make you feel comfortable and at ease. You will digest your food much easier and healthier.

49. **CREATE AN UPLIFTING ARRAY OF DIFFERENT TASTES SENSATIONS** for your taste buds! Include sweet, sour, salty, astringent, bitter and pungent foods into your nourish routine daily.

50. **NOURISH YOUR MIND. NOURISH YOUR RELATIONSHIP. NOURISH YOUR BODY. NOURISH YOUR SOUL.**

Believe

1. **IT ALL STARTS WITH BELIEVE.** You can't live a positive life with a negative mind. Once you have a handle on believe it opens up a whole world of possibilities.

2. **FOCUS ON THE POSITIVE:** Choose to focus on the positive aspects in your life by learning what you love and cherish the most. Get a pen and paper and write a list of the 10 things in your life that you LOVE and appreciate most. See aren't you lucky?

3. **MAKE A BELIEVE BOARD.** A visual representation of your best life possible. Conceptulise. Collect. Categorise. Arrange. Compose. It's time to spark up the laws of attraction.

4. **STOP AND THINK DOES IT REALLY MATTER?** Does it really matter if you have to bend down and pick up the papers you dropped, if you miss your bus or your mobile phone breaks? I think you will find that most times, it doesn't really matter and most things can be fixed. So take it all in your stride and don't let the little things weigh you down.

5. **SEND YOUR MUM OR BEST FRIEND FLOWERS – JUST BECAUSE.**

6. **LAUGH YOURSELF SILLY.** In a study of 54,000 people by a Norwegian university, subjects who scored top in humour appreciation were 35 percent more likely to survive when hit with a serious disease.

7. **ASK YOURSELF…CAN I DO SOMETHING ABOUT IT?** If you are living with anxiety, sift through your thoughts and pinpoint what it is that is effecting you. If it should turn out that it matters, be sure to consider if there is anything you can do about it, right now! If there is, then life is too short to dwell, go ahead and do it and make amends, and if there isn't, what's the use of letting it get to you?

8. **DON'T LET MOMENTS PASS YOU BY.** Be present and take the time to enjoy special moments before they pass.

9. **KEEP YOUR COOL.** If you are at ease, you put others at ease, which makes for a relaxed social atmosphere.

10. **TO QUOTE OSCAR WILDE: BE YOURSELF – EVERYONE ELSE IS ALREADY TAKEN.**

11. **SURROUND YOURSELF WITH PEOPLE YOU LOVE** that believe in you and will only criticise when they think it is genuinely in your best interests.

12. **VIEW SETBACKS AS AN OPPORTUNITY** to test yourself and push ahead to achieve more.

13. **EVERY DAY IS A NEW START.** If you slip up, be kind to yourself. There's always another day.

14. **PARTICIPATE IN RANDOM ACTS OF KINDNESS.** When you are present in any act of giving kindness or simply offering thanks to others, your happy chemicals in your brain go into overdrive, or in scientific terms those all-important serotonin levels rise. Talk about spreading the love!

15. **DON'T GIVE OUT - OR ACCEPT - BLAME EASILY.**

16. **MAKE SMALL CHANGES TO REAP BIG REWARDS.** It's about progress not perfection.

17. **QUIT PICKING ON YOURSELF.** We all make mistakes. That's life. Instead of punishing yourself, view every mishap as a gift to grow.

18. **DO WHAT YOU LOVE, AND DO IT OFTEN.** Every day, do at least one thing for you. Whether it's going for a walk in nature, sitting and having a cup of herbal tea, calling your bestie, doing yoga, meditating, whatever it is…do something that YOU love.

19. **PRACTISE THE ART OF FORGIVENESS.** Whether it be forgiving yourself or somebody else. Forgiveness is the key to freedom and happiness. Set yourself free and forgive today.

20. **SILENCE IS YOUR FRIEND.** Sitting in silence is the best way to calm and quiet the mind.

21. **KEEP A GRATITUDE JOURNAL.** It will help put things in perspective.

22. **WHEN YOU WAKE UP MAKE SURE THE FIRST THOUGHT YOU THINK IS A POSITIVE ONE.**

23. **COVER YOUR WORKSPACE** in inspiration, words of wisdom, art you love and photographs you cherish.

24. **GET OUT OF YOUR COMFORT ZONE EVERY ONCE IN A WHILE**.

25. **MAKE A PINTEREST BOARD** to act as your online visual manifestation.

26. **PRACTISE MINDFULNESS.**

27. **DETOXIFY YOURSELF OF NEGATIVE RELATIONSHIPS.**

28. **REMINDER: EVERYTHING IS BEAUTIFUL BUT NOT EVERYONE SEES IT.**

29. **WEAR YOUR LORNA JANE INSPIRATIONAL SINGLET** to get you through the toughest of times.

30. **STAY TRUE TO YOU** and you will end up blissfully HAPPY.

31. **THINK HAPPY, BE HAPPY.**

32. **THE ESSENTIALS TO LIVING A HAPPY LIFE ARE:** Something to do, something to love and something to hope for.

33. **GET YOUR DIY ON.** It's time to get crafty and learn a new skill.

34. **IMMERSE YOURSELF** in riveting reads that challenge and educate you.

35. **WHY FIT IN WHEN YOU WERE BORN TO STAND OUT?** Individuality is an empowering thing, so embrace it!

36. **KEEP YOUR VISIONS ALIVE.** How? By thought, by reminders in your room, screensavers on your iPhone and by surrounding yourself with people who will inspire and encourage you to reach them.

37. **KNOW YOUR SIMPLE TRUTHS.** As a woman, it is easy to forget the simple truths like, 'I am beautiful', 'I have purpose', 'I am blessed', 'I am unique' and 'I am enough'. These simple truths are plagued with negative thoughts from society at large. We lose sight of our true potential. This is why it's so imperative to have truth in yourself and your beliefs. Try to eliminate the negativity, and start believing in what is true about YOU!

38. **DON'T LET DISAPPOINTMENT STOP YOU!** Start looking at disappointment in a new light; think of it not as a set back but rather encouragement to defy the odds and achieve your dreams! It's a true fighter that gets back up when they have been knocked down.

39. **BE A CHEERLEADER.** Instead of putting yourself in the centre of your universe, become a cheerleader to applaud and encourage others in your life.

40. **QUIT COMPARING.** As we all know, 'comparison is the thief of joy and it is this kind of view in life that can destruct our beliefs.

41. **STRIVE FOR CONTENTMENT.** Being content with what you have is a skill that is hard to acquire in life. It is crucial to acknowledge who we are. Teach yourself daily things to be grateful for, and change the view from your cup being half empty to half full.

42. **MAKE A LOVE LIST.** Write down a list of things you love about yourself, and read it at times when you are feeling down.

43. **FIND YOUR SWEET SPOT.** A place you can go to be one with your thoughts and totally at peace.

44. **PRACTISE THE ART OF MEDITATION.**

45. **FIND YOURSELF A LIFE COACH/MENTOR** who can point you in the right direction.

46. **MIRROR WORK.** Get comfortable in front of a mirror and repeat positive affirmations like "I love and accept myself."

47. **SET YOURSELF SMART GOALS.** Remember to be specific, measurable, attainable, realistic and tangible.

48. **DON'T BE AFRAID TO DAYDREAM.** It is an absolute necessity for the mind and spirit to have the freedom to explore new possibilities or revisit dreams that are deep within the heart.

49. **EXPRESS YOURSELF THROUGH CREATIVITY.**

50. **NEVER NEVER NEVER GIVE UP**.

For MORE inspiration visit
MOVENOURISHBELIEVE.COM

KEEP
CALM
AND
MNB

YOU LOOK
**AMAZING
TODAY**
MOVE NOURISH BELIEVE

NOURISH

JUST
DO
SQUATS

TAKE MORE
CHANCES.
DANCE MORE
DANCES.

WHEN
was the
last time
you did
something
for the
first time

your active life starts here

YOU
ARE GOOD
ENOUGH.

Love Lorna + Roger

Thank you

First and foremost I would like to thank all of the women who love and support Lorna Jane - you are the reason we exist and my daily inspiration to not only design great active wear but to promote Active Living and the joyous life it represents.

Special Thanks to:

My husband Bill.
My amazing family and friends.
My inspiring team at Lorna Jane and especially those who worked lovingly on this book: Tara, Ash, Rhi, Shaelah, Lauren, Jenna, Grace, Davina, Emily, Steph, Laura, Christina and Sofie.

And of course the delightful girls at Messenger Group.

"IN THE END
WE ONLY
REGRET
THE CHANCES
WE DIDN'T
TAKE."

~ *Lorna Jane*